Bird

Bird Sounds

HOW AND WHY BIRDS SING, CALL, CHATTER, AND SCREECH

Barry Kent MacKay

STACKPOLE
BOOKS

Published by
STACKPOLE BOOKS
5067 Ritter Road
Mechanicsburg, PA 17055
www.stackpolebooks.com

Printed in China

Cover design by Tracy Patterson
Cover painting by Barry Kent MacKay

10 9 8 7 6 5 4 3 2 1

First edition

Library of Congress Cataloging-in-Publication Data
MacKay, Barry Kent, 1943-
      Bird Sounds/Barry MacKay.—1st ed.
         p.   cm
      ISBN 0-8117-2787-4
      1. Birdsongs. 2. Birds—Vocalization. I. Title.
QL698.5 .M33 2001
598.159′4—dc21

                                   00-032957

CONTENTS

ACKNOWLEDGMENTS

There is no one line of demarcation or firm criterion I can think of that would fairly distinguish between those people who selflessly assisted me in the direct preparation of the current volume, and those, some no longer with us, whose help was instrumental to the knowledge and interest I brought to the project. I apologize to those in both categories who are not mentioned here and to whom I owe so much. Writing is not as lonely a process as sometimes made out to be, and while I accept sole responsibility for errors committed in the text, it was only through the assistance of others that I could attempt a text on such a technical and multi-faceted subject as bird sound.

Lifetime friend Ronald I. Orenstein kindly contributed far beyond what was requested in reviewing virtually all of the text, making significant suggestions as to changes that invariably improved it, and in drawing upon his own prodigious knowledge of ornithological lore to correct some major errors and provide better examples of characteristics being described. My bird-loving mother, Phyllis E. MacKay, has always contributed support for her wayward son's unrelenting devotion to birds, up to and including the preparations of text and art for this volume. I am deeply in debt to the continued kindness of the staff, past and present, of the ornithology department of the Royal Ontario Museum, in Toronto, where Mark K. Peck, Ross James, Allan J. Baker, Glenn B. Murphy, and Jon C. Barlow have supported this and similar endeavors by providing necessary information and reference materials and welcome advice. James A. Rising, of the Department of Zoology, University of Toronto, and Martin C. Michener, of MIST Software Associates, in Hollis, New Hampshire, both kindly read and productively commented on specific areas of text. Alan Berger, Dena Jones, and other friends and colleagues at the Animal Protection Institute, in Sacramento, California, assisted by allowing the kind of flexibility required to be able to take on this project. Also in Sacramento are Bruce Webb and Tim Manolis and their respective families, who have done so much to allow me to greatly enhance my knowledge of and experience with the birds of the western U.S. and who are here acknowledged both for their own kindnesses and to symbolize many more field companions with whom I've shared time birding in various corners of the globe. The International Crane Foundation, in Baraboo, Wisconsin, kindly allowed me to experience the vocalizations of Whooping Cranes at close proximity. I am grateful to my agent, Frances Hanna, of Acacia Publishing House, for smoothing over for me all business details, and to my long-suffering editors at Stackpole, for their patience, good humor, and understanding as I grappled with unexpected delays.

AUTHOR'S NOTE

About the time the text of this book was begun, news broke of an experiment conducted by Dr. Kevin Long, of the Neurosciences Unit in La Jolla, California. Long had, to put it simply, transplanted embryonic brain tissue from a quail into a chicken. According to earlier reports, such experiments had caused the recipient chicken to vocalize and make head movements in the manner of the quail. The more recent effort, involving material taken from the anterior midbrain of the quail, produced a "chimeric" chicken (from "chimera," meaning a mixed species) that responded to the call of a hen quail in preference to the call of the hen chicken.

About the time the manuscript for this book was completed, there were new reports about research on the brain of the late Albert Einstein. Einstein, whose name has become synonymous with genius, died in 1955, at the age of 76, leaving his brain to science. Forty-four years later, Dr. Sandra Witelson, working at McMaster University, in Hamiton, Ontario, announced that comparisons of the configuration of Einstein's brain with many other human brains indicated that there might have been a physiological difference that accounted for Einstein's genius. Put in very simple terms, it seemed that the part of the brain that controls math ability was better developed in Einstein than in the rest of us. The inferior parietal region, believed to be at the seat of mathematical ability, was 15 percent wider on both sides within Einstein's brain than is average for human brains. "This indicates," said Witelson at the time, "there may be an anatomical basis for differences in intelligence. But it shouldn't be seen as 'anatomy is destiny.' Environment has a very important role to play in learning and brain development."

In between these two news events, as I was writing the text, I found myself submerged in a wide and fascinating variety of scientific studies and popularized texts published to help us better understand the nature of sound, both mechanical and vocal, produced by birds. It was an exploration that followed a lifetime love for birds that owed much to sheer, uncritical fascination. The two approaches are not necessarily the same. Partly I have always been an admirer of birds, anxious to see them, paint them, and care for them. And partly I have been fascinated by how they function, driven by a need to better understand them. I have acted not entirely through reductionist procedures that isolate, catalog, and quantify aspects of birds and their behavior, nor entirely as romanticist, satisfied to accept at subjective face value only the visible surface of "birdness." In a sense, I feel chimerical, myself, with the fascination for the mechanistic reply to the "how" and "why" of things co-existing with the anthropomorphic instincts I felt as a young child totally captivated by what the late American bird artist, Louis Agassiz Fuertes, called "the singular beauty of birds."

There are times, reading the text, when it may seem that birds are mere automatons, reacting without conscience or will to forces from within and without that form the boundaries of their very nature. But they are far more than that, these fellow beings that enrich the lives of so many of us. As I worked on this book, I followed developments in other studies that indicated that birds were "more intelligent" than previously thought. There are those of us who never had any doubts. Not that it matters; what matters is that the value of birds, like that of all creatures, is inherent unto themselves as wondrous manifestations of this world's great legacy of life, in all its variety of form and shades of splendor.

This volume would not be possible without the work—often done under arduous conditions, and sometimes involving lifetimes—of numerous scientists and naturalists, in the field and in the laboratory, who made it their business to learn about birds. Throughout the following text you will see such phrases as "Scientists have found" or "Research has shown" or "Studies reveal" followed by information. That does not make me the author of that information. I am merely a conduit of knowledge acquired by others. For the sake of narrative flow, those others often remain anonymous within these pages, and I regret that. Much of what I relate was learned recently by scientists, some of them friends, as growth in natural sciences is exponential, fanning out to probe ever more into the nature of species even as we lose them at rates unprecedented since the loss of the dinosaurs. Study is ongoing around the world, and interpreters such as myself, fascinated by what others learn, seek to convey the exciting essence of new, complex, and evolving knowledge and try, at times imperfectly, to provide the historic context based on work of earlier observers, including those gifted with prescient inspiration, seeing what others might have seen, but understanding so much more. It is my hope that from the growing body of knowledge of nature comes the combination of wisdom and compassion that may be necessary if we are to better harmonize our relations with this planet, currently so abused, and the beings with whom we so intrusively coexist. For all that I love or am fascinated by nature, I must first declare myself to be a conservationist.

I hope that for you, as for me, there comes a moment, perhaps in the stillness of the night when ground mists glow silvery in starlight, when a Screech-Owl calls and the science retreats, if just a little, and the magic can be heard.

Barry Kent MacKay
Markham, Ontario

ONE

An Introduction to Bird Sound

The jungle was dense with humidity. Masses of great trees, thick vines, and complicated colonies of epiphytes, orchids, and ferns were dimly visible. Dull, gray-gold shafts of uncertain light probed the tropical rain forest.

My eyes, though adjusted to the dark, separated out little form or structure. There were unidentified odors of soil and life lingering after the night's rainfall. What dominated my senses, though, was a cacophony of exotic sounds all around. Apart from the strident *ca-CA-caw; ca-CA-caw* of Mealy Parrots, there were few sounds I could identify on this, my first morning in a tropical rain forest.

I had slept poorly, thinking of the rich assortment of life in the nearby Costa Rican forest, and now I was awake in the bleak grayness, with the sky lightening overhead. I couldn't always distinguish among frogs, insects, birds, or possibly mammals. Peeps, whistles, croaks, gurgles, screeches, and sharply defined, whistled phrases competed for my attention as I fought to sort the sounds and find an order to them, and planned to find their authors as the daylight intensified.

That morning of discovery was followed by others, and slowly an increasing degree of familiarity developed. I heard the rapid tapping of a Rufous-winged Woodpecker. A clear, musical whistle I traced to a White-breasted Wood-Wren; such a small bird to make so loud, clear, and fine a whistle. A soft, weak, and somewhat nasal call note led me to a pair of Black-crowned Tityras near their nest cavity in an overhead tree limb. A guttural sound left me mystified until much searching of the overhead canopy revealed a red blob that soon resolved itself into the lower breast of a Slaty-tailed Trogon. From grassy clearings came the thin and variable trills of the ubiquitous Yellow-faced Grassquit. A strange barking sound confused me for days until at last I discovered that it was the call of a Gray-headed Kite, perched in the forest canopy. But other sounds remained mysterious, uttered by species unknown.

Vocal Sounds

When you think of the sounds birds make, you probably first think of familiar ones such as the singing of robins or canaries, or perhaps the raucous cawing of a crow. Such avian vocalizations are produced differently from our own.

Sound occurs when something vibrates air, or another medium, setting up a wave that is translated into sound by our hearing apparatus. Vocalization implies the passage of air up through an organism's breathing apparatus and out into the open. How the air is modified on its way out determines the qualities of the sound produced.

What information the vocalization conveys depends on how it is perceived or interpreted by the listener. When another person speaks, unless we know the language, we may receive very little information. Individual words or gestures may mean different things to different people. Sometimes we may communicate without language, knowing that a person is fearful, happy, or angry.

Vocalization also implies that the air is forced and modified to achieve something more than the quiet sound of breathing. We draw in extra breath before speaking and modify it as we exhale in a controlled manner. The number of consecutive words we can say is limited to the amount of breath we can exhale before having to refill our lungs and replenish our oxygen. Birds have no such limitation.

Vocalization may be little more than hissing or sighing. That is about all the vocalization some birds, such as the King Vulture of tropical America, are capable of producing. Most bird species are capable of enough modification of the outgoing column of air to produce a distinctive sound, ranging from a simple one-note call, squeak, or croak to long, intricate, and musical songs of extraordinary extravagance and complexity.

Birds communicate and hear at higher frequencies, on average, than do humans. Songbirds, particularly, tend to communicate and hear at a level between 2,000 and 4,000 hertz, a measurement indicating the number of vibrations occurring within a unit of time. Most humans can hear at the same level as birds but communicate within the lower reaches of that range, whereas birds tend to communicate at the higher reaches.

Mechanical Sounds

For mechanical sounds to occur, there still needs to be the act of producing vibration, as when one object hits another. Sometimes the object that is hit is the air itself, producing a sound wave. The most obvious example of this is the sound of wings beating against air. Mechanical sound may involve rattling the mandibles of the beak together, striking an object with the beak, vibrating wing or tail feathers, or using elaborate anatomical adaptations. It may be something as simple as splashing water, which can serve to distract a predator. The Black Palm Cockatoo has taken mechanical sound production to a higher level of sophistication by using a small branch to strike a larger one to produce true drumming. It may be the only species that uses a tool to produce a noise, although woodpeckers drum with their beaks. The region the Black Palm Cockatoo inhabits has no woodpeckers.

When a pheasant, quail, dove, or grouse explodes into flight from cover, the sound of rapidly beating wings may startle, and therefore confuse, an approaching predator. The whistling of wings of flocking waterfowl or shorebirds may serve to keep the group together or even convey slight changes in speed or direction to other flock members. The more nocturnal owl species have fringes around the edges of their primary flight feathers, rendering their flight quieter than it would be if the feathers had crisp edges.

The suggestion has been made by some naturalists that the splash of an Osprey or a Belted Kingfisher seeking prey near the water's surface has a stunning effect on small fish, rendering them more vulnerable. I've watched large flocks of American Coots splash noisily as they pattered off in all directions or dived in response to the swoop of a Bald Eagle, the splashing apparently serving to distract the predator. The male European Coot, perched on the edge of his nest or a piece of flotsam, will slap the water with his broadly scalloped toes, the splash serving to challenge rival males while advertising his presence to prospective mates.

Although the functions of many mechanical sounds are known, other sound-producing behavior remains unexplained. By closely observing the reactions a bird's sound production generates, we may develop an increasing understanding of the complex role of bird sound in avian social behavior and survival techniques.

TWO

How Birds Sing

Dappled blotches of gold-toned sunlight contrasted with deep green shades and glittering white highlights where sunlight was shattered by a leaf. All around, coastal redwood trees towered majestically as I stood on a narrow switchback footpath on the edge of a deep canyon in the California coastal range. Far below, a crystalline stream gurgled seaward. All around me, I could hear the songs of Winter Wrens, tumbling like the water in the stream, cleaving through dark shadows and hidden places. Occasionally I could glimpse one of the singers—tiny, mouselike birds that seemed impossibly small to be authors of such long and complex songs. Not for the first time, I allowed myself to be lost in admiration of this wonderful gift, the song a perfect counterpoint to this forest, and to all the wild and beautiful places throughout so much of North America, Europe, and Asia, where this tiny bird sings.

Let us consider the songbird as a musical instrument. There must be something that vibrates in a musical instrument, whether it is the head of a drum, the reed of a clarinet, or the string of a harp plucked by the musician's fingers. What causes the vibrations in a bird—as in our own bodies when we speak, sing, whistle, cough, or sneeze—are selected parts of the body itself.

At the junction of the trachea and the bronchial tubes is a structure, called the syrinx, that is unique to birds. In some species, the syrinx is little more than an enlargement of the trachea, but in songbirds, the syrinx has a boxlike shape. Muscles that control it make changes in the shape of selected parts of the syrinx in ways we are only beginning to understand. Their workings are the key to the incredible complexity and diversity of birdsong.

In songbirds, the syrinx is formed in part from the trachea and in part from the upper ends of the primary bronchi. Imagine a column of air moving from deeper within the bird, up through the bronchi, and through the syrinx. What happens to each part of that column of air determines the nature of the sound produced.

At the base of the syrinx is a chamber with connections to the interclavicular air sac. Air passing through this chamber brushes one side of a very thin, taut membrane called the internal tympaniform membrane, or *membrana tympaniformis interna*. Small projections lie on either side of the passages through which the air passes as it flows up the bronchi and into the syrinx. Each of those on the outer side of the passage is called an external labium, and each of the corresponding internal projections is called an internal labium. The internal labia act on the air both in the bronchi and in the interclavicular air sac. These tiny features can change their configuration to minute degrees in fractions of seconds, and in so doing, modify the vibrations of the air column to establish the characteristics of the sound it produces—at least in part. Until recent studies indicated otherwise, it was assumed that sound was primarily produced by the vibrations of the tympaniform membrane. New studies indicate that the membrane is primarily a support structure; it is rapid and precise changes in the thickness and configuration of the labia that are primarily responsible, within the trachea,

As with all songbirds, the Song Thrush, of Europe, has a well-developed syrinx (at left, see text) that delicately and rapidly controls minute changes in airflow to produce its song.

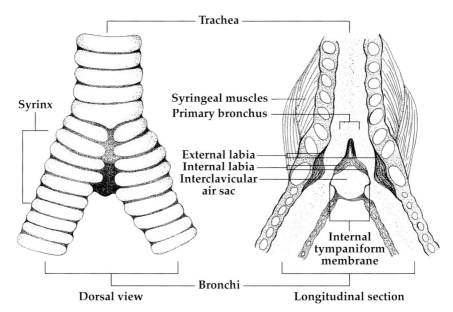

Cross section of a syrinx   Line Drawing by Shelly Hawley-Yan "On Dragon Wings"

for sound production. Experts have determined that humans use only about 2 percent of the air column that passes out of the respiratory system in making vocalizations, whereas songbirds use nearly 100 percent of the air column to produce song.

Another source of change to the configuration of the space through which the air passes is the interclavicular air sac. It surrounds the syrinx, and as pressure within it increases, the membranes that must vibrate to create sound are pushed into the air column. If the interclavicular air sac is punctured, song cannot occur.

It is in the songbirds, or oscines, that there is the greatest anatomical adaptation to manipulate vocal sound production in order to produce sustained and variable song. Our musical instrument, then, is possessed of a music box whose complexity and detail scientists are only beginning to discover.

Air: Source of Sound

As air is the medium of sound transmission, some understanding of the bird's respiratory system is necessary. Birds' lungs are fixed in place as relatively small, bright pink organs of spongelike tissue full of openings and pockets through which air passes. They have more air openings than the lungs of mammals; in fact, they have relatively equal surface area at half the size of mammalian lungs. Air can only go into or out of the mammal lung, whereas it passes through the avian lung. Distributed through it, the bird has a number of bubble-like, thin-walled sacs made of transparent tissue. From the lungs, the air sacs extend to various parts of the body. There are anywhere from six to fourteen different air sacs, depending on the species, but most birds have nine, varying in shape to fit the contours of the bird's body.

A bird may breathe in and out as rapidly as two times a second, or a little more, in the case of a hummingbird, although a large bird may breathe at about the same rate as we do at similar stages of exertion or rest. ■

The nine air sacs usually found in birds include two on either side of the neck called the cervical air sacs. These are what one sees inflated in the visually striking display of the frigatebird. Male frigatebirds inflate the sacs into great balloon shapes that occupy the area between the chin and throat. The outer skin covering of the sacs is bright red. It looks as though such a pent-up volume of air could be used to make a terrific bag-pipelike sound, but apart from some occasional bill rattling, the display is quite silent.

Moving toward the rear of the bird, next are the anterior (front) thoracic air sacs, which occupy the forepart of the bird's body. Then come the posterior (rear) thoracic air sacs, which occupy the upper chest of the bird. On the rear underside of the bird, in the area of the belly, there is a pair of large abdominal sacs.

Between the shoulder blades, a single interclavicular air sac connects to the hollow interiors of the wing bones, possibly the sternum, and most importantly for sound production, it reaches up to where the syrinx is located. Together, the air sacs and their various extensions, or diverticula, constitute about 80 percent of the volume of the bird's entire respiratory system.

Some air sacs may extend into some of the smaller bones, again depending on species. Generally, large aquatic birds have the most pneumatized, or air-filled, skeletons, although some, like loons and penguins, have dense bones that make these birds less buoyant, facilitating their underwater pursuit of fish.

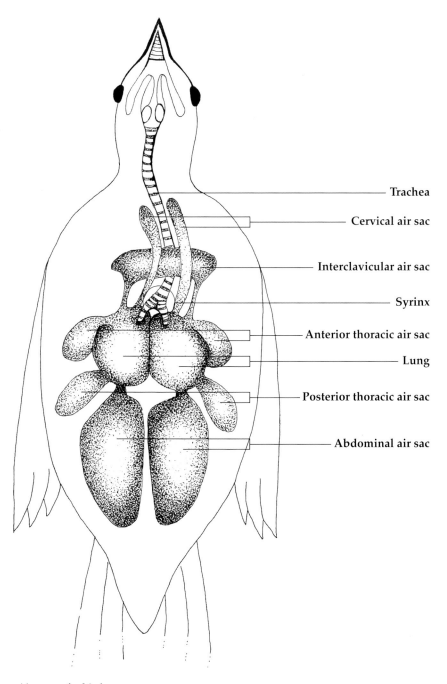

Trachea

Cervical air sac

Interclavicular air sac

Syrinx

Anterior thoracic air sac

Lung

Posterior thoracic air sac

Abdominal air sac

Air sacs of a bird   LINE DRAWING BY SHELLY HAWLEY-YAN "ON DRAGON WINGS"

Birds have high metabolisms, creating high temperatures. The air sacs function, in part, as a cooling system by transmitting heat from the body to air that is usually cooler than the bird's body temperature—a biological precursor to the air-cooled engine. But the air sacs, along with the lungs, are sources of air with which to make sound.

Birds' breathing is quite fundamental to vocal sound production, and very different from how humans breathe. Birds lack a diaphragm—a sheet of tissue that separates the abdomen from the thorax in mammals. Instead, the whole body cavity of birds expands with the lowering of the sternum

Cycle One

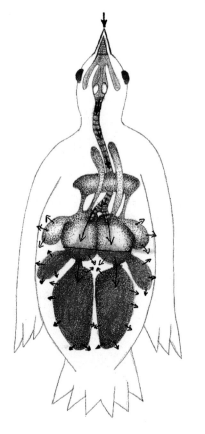
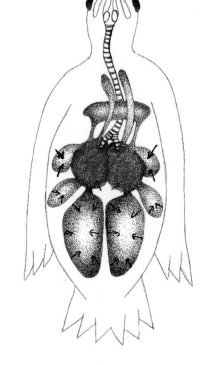

Inspiration   **Expiration**

Bird respiration   Line Drawing by Shelly Hawley-Yan "On Dragon Wings"

(the large "breast bone" that occupies most of the chest area of birds) and the expansion of the rib cage outward. Air sacs and lungs expand enough to bring air into the bird's body through the nostrils and mouth, through the sinuses and nasal cavities, and down the trachea into an intricate network of passageways consisting of the lungs and air sacs. The efficiency of air exchange is significantly higher in birds than in mammals, with virtually all the air in the lungs replaced by each breath or, to be more precise, with every two breaths, as two inhalations and two exhalations are required to produce one complete exchange of air.

Cycle Two

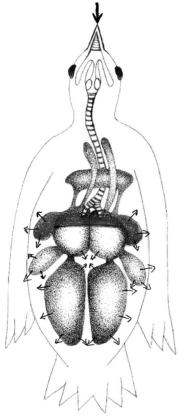 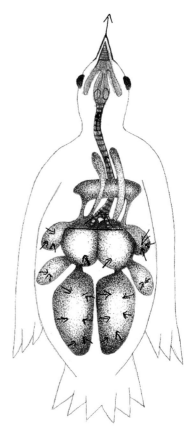

Inspiration   **Expiration**

If we could follow a given breath, we would find that our instrument is a little more sophisticated than, say, a bagpipe, where the air is blown by the piper into a large bag and then squeezed out—not unlike the process that allows humans to speak or sing, except that, as is true of the bird but not us, the breath may be stored for more than one cycle of inhalation and exhalation. Initially, the puff of air does not go directly into the lungs, but passes through them without gas exchange. The puff of air first goes to the rear part of the bird's body. First, most of the air the bird inhales reaches the posterior air sacs, including the large, paired abdominal air sacs. Parts of the lungs also receive air, and there is a subsequent exchange of gases as the breath passes through the lungs on the way to the back of the bird. But as the bird breathes out, the posterior air sacs contract, pushing the puff of air into the lungs, completing the first cycle of the bird's two-step breathing process.

As the bird breathes in again, while new air enters the bird via the route just described, the initial puff exits most of the lungs and enters the anterior air sacs via lung bronchi, where more gas exchange occurs. This single breath of air carries with it some of the warmth generated by the bird's metabolic

Definitions used to describe sound tend to be rather circular and complex, although most of us, through music, have an intuitive grasp of what the terminology refers to. Sound is caused by vibrations, which produce variations in pressure of the medium (usually air) through which sound travels. These variations are referred to as sound waves. The quality and characteristics of the sound are determined by numerous factors. The faster the vibration, the higher the frequency, and the higher-pitched the sound becomes. Frequency is measured in how many thousands of cycles occur in one second, with 1,000 cycles equaling 1 kilohertz (kHz). Pitch is the placement of a tone within a scale, determined by frequency. Tone is a clear sound of specific pitch and quality. Tone is, according to my dictionary, "a musical sound of definite pitch, consisting of several relatively simple constituents called partial tones, the lowest of which is called the fundamental tone and the others harmonies or overtones."

continued on page 13

Loudness, or amplitude, is a measurement of the degree of pressure imposed upon the air by the source of the vibrations. A foghorn may produce a very low sound in terms of pitch but a very loud sound in terms of amplitude. Conversely, a Blackpoll Warbler's song may be very high in pitch but have little amplitude. It can therefore be heard from only a fraction of the distance that we can hear the foghorn. The amplitude is usually expressed by a logarithmic measurement of sound pressure, called a decibel (dB), for a tenth of a bel (deci, meaning one tenth, and bel, the log to the base ten of the sound pressure). If the sound pressure is 1,000, there are 3 bels, or 30 decibels; if it is 1,000,000, you have 6 bels, or 60 dB. In fact, decibels are always given relative to a reference level, usually the threshold of human hearing at optimum frequency, which is around 400 Hz. Since it is the high frequencies people find irritating, sound measurements for environmental studies are always weighted to discount the readings on low-pitched sound. This is known as "A" weighting, and the results are therefore abbreviated as dBA, often seen on Environmental Impact Statements pertaining to such things as the building of new highways or airports or the sound levels in workplaces. Standing next to a foghorn when it blows can be a shattering experience, and prolonged exposure to such high decibels can be damaging to the ear. But standing next to a Blackpoll Warbler in full song is as harmless an experience as it is pleasant. ◼

processes, which normally maintain a body temperature a few degrees higher than that of a human (about 42 to 44 degrees Celsius when active, compared to approximately 37 degrees Celsius in humans). The air puff contains carbon dioxide in exchange for the oxygen required to fuel metabolism. The body contracts, and the initial puff of air leaves via the anterior air sacs at the front of the bird and the bronchial tubes that lead up from the lungs past the point where they join the trachea, and out. Put simply, the same breath of air passes through the lungs twice, although not the same parts of the lungs.

As he sings, the throat of the Song Sparrow, one of North America's most widely distributed bird species, pulses in accompaniment to a complex range of rapidly uttered notes.

Now let us back up a little and try to visualize a small section of the songbird's internal mechanisms. Extending through the front of each of its two lungs is a short tube called a primary *bronchus* (the singular form of bronchi). These bronchi, also called bronchial tubes, come together at the base of the trachea, or windpipe, which leads up to the mouth cavity. At that intersection is the syrinx. Even after the air passes through the syrinx, it is still modified further by the pulsating throat and small changes in head posture and mouth opening. If you watch a domestic canary or a Song Sparrow in full song, you may see the throat pulsate vigorously and the mouth open to varying degrees as the emerging column of air is influenced by each tiny change in configuration and positioning of the upper end of the respiratory system.

THREE

Songbirds

Because the term *songbird* implies an ability to sing (and perhaps, as well, that nonsongbirds must therefore be nonsingers), it is not as popular among ornithologists and experienced birders as the more correct Passeriformes. Equally correct is the use of the term *passerine*, which can be used as an adjective or a noun. The word is from the Latin *passer*, meaning "sparrow," and *forma*, meaning "form"—thus, sparrow-shaped.

A songbird is a member of the order Passeriformes. An order is made up of one or more families sharing various characteristics, and a family consists of one or more species sharing various characteristics.

Within the Passeriformes there are two suborders. One is oscines (pronounced O-sci-nees or ah-seens) and the other is labeled suboscine. The term *oscine* derives from the Latin *oscen*, plural *oscines*, and means a singing bird, particularly used in *aupicies*, which is an ancient custom of divination from the examination of birds' entrails, flight patterns, or voices. Some ornithologists reserve the term songbird exclusively for the oscines. The suboscines may have the more ancient lineage, dating back before the Miocene epoch, which began approximately 25 million years ago and saw the first appearance of oscines in increasing numbers of species.

Songbirds have been enormously successful as a group. Approximately three-fifths of all bird species are classified as songbirds. Songbirds are found on every continent except Antarctica, although some species do occur on rugged islands in the high latitudes of the Southern Hemisphere, well within the ice-chilled influence of the Antarctic. Songbirds occur near the tops of the highest peaks and in the high latitudes of the Arctic, although they attain the greatest diversity of species in tropical rain forests. By far the greatest numbers of suboscine families and species are found in tropical America.

The various oscine species range in size from the tiny Pygmy Tit of Java (estimated to weigh around 3 or 4 grams; I am not sure that anyone has ever weighed one) to the Thick-billed Raven of the Ethiopian highlands (which has been estimated to weigh somewhere around 1,500 to 2,000 grams or more, although it appears that it, too, has never had its weight recorded). In North America, the smallest songbird is the Bushtit, weighing in at 5 or 6 grams, or perhaps the Golden-crowned Kinglet, which may weigh 4 to 6.5 grams, while the largest is the Common Raven, tipping the scales at 920 to 1,560 grams.

Suboscines

Suboscines have no more than four pairs of muscles that manipulate the syrinx to make sound. Members of one small family of suboscines, the New Zealand Wrens (which are not wrens—true wrens are oscines), have no muscles controlling the syrinx. As might be assumed, their "songs" are simple calls, squeaks, or trills. Oscines have five to eight pairs of muscles that control the configuration of the syrinx to produce vocalizations and are generally much more musical than the suboscines.

Something of an exception to all this are the two species of lyrebirds, oscines native to Australia. They have a syrinx with only three pairs of attached intrinsic muscles, whereas other oscines have more—up to eight pairs. In common with another oscine, the scrubbird (also of Australia), these muscles are attached differently than in other oscines. Here they are attached to the extremities of the bronchial semirings, support structures that partly surround and support the bronchial tubes, and thus these birds are classified as Acromyodian passerines, from *acro,* meaning "extremity" or "tip." The Superb Lyrebird is a wondrous mimic, quite capable of imitating the complexities of songs of neighboring oscines with more complex vocal systems with such fidelity that birds and birders alike cannot tell the mimicker from the mimicked.

The songs of the suboscines are essentially hard-wired and unchanging—they do not need to be learned—while the oscines' songs are partly inherent (the template upon which the song normally is constructed) and partly the result of experience, having been learned. The suboscines generally do not vary their songs, as do the oscines, and typically do not modify them under outside influences. Suboscines include such families as tyrant flycatchers, cotingas, antbirds, manakins, and Neotropical ovenbirds. Although most species are found in Central and South America, there are many species of tyrant flycatchers in North America, including such familiar species as kingbirds, phoebes, and wood-pewees. In the Old World, there are three families of birds traditionally classified as sub-oscines, two almost completely restricted to the tropics and subtropics of the Ethiopian, Oriental, and Australasian faunal regions, and one confined to New Zealand.

The Oscine Song

The structure of oscine song can range from a simple, single note to a complex, harmonic blend of multiple tones. A tone is a single sound of a specific pitch. Harmonics, also called overtones, contain a number of frequencies. Frequency is a measurement of vibrations in a given unit of time, usually expressed as hertz and kilohertz. A low, bass note of 90 hertz, for example, as found in the low whistle of a Spruce Grouse, may be compared to the thin, high sound of a singing Blackpoll Warbler, at 9 kilohertz, or nine times 1,000 cycles per second. Both species occur in the black spruce boreal forests of North America.

The manner in which harmonics are combined contributes to the overall quality and timbre of the sound. The lowest of the tones—the one produced with the most energy—constituting the sound is called the fundamental frequency. Other tones within the call are multiples of the fundamental frequency. The subjectively pleasing sound of a Hermit Thrush derives from emphasis on the odd-numbered harmonics. Such sound seems pleasing, similarly to the way the blended voices of a choir are pleasing. Other combinations may produce relatively harsh or grating sounds. The pleasing quality we attribute to the song of the Nightingale or the Wood Thrush would not be possible without the bird's ability to harmonize disparate song elements.

In birds, the fundamental is seldom the loudest. In such species as the widely known Red-breasted Nuthatch, the fundamental is inaudible; only the overtones—the harmonics, exact whole integer multiples of the fundamental—can be heard. For example, for a Red-breasted Nuthatch song, the fundamental is 500 Hz, and only the third through ninth harmonics are audible, visible in the spectrum. That is what makes these energetic little birds sound like "tiny trumpets"—real trumpets do this too.

Singing Two Songs as One

Some oscines, such as the Brown Thrasher, native to North America, actually have two songs, sung simultaneously. Each is distinct from the other. They emerge from the bird's throat as a single song, but a sonogram

reveals two separate and independent vocalizations, not only uttered by the same bird, but blended into a harmonic whole. The bird's control of the configuration of the syrinx and associated sound-producing anatomy is so finely tuned that it can operate one side of the syrinx independently of the other. By rapidly altering the configuration of the trachea, throat, and mouth, the bird can focus the two separate elements into the single complete song. Like a pianist's two hands playing tune and harmony, a bird can blend two separate sounds into a pleasing harmonic. This ability has also been discovered in suboscines and in various nonpasseriform species, including waterfowl, herons, and shorebirds, although with considerably less complexity than displayed by oscine virtuosos.

Use of Sound to Communicate

Birds, like other animals, can use acoustic, visual, chemical, or tactile means of communication. Sound and visual communication are the two methods that birds most often use to communicate to each other. Most birds have little or no sense of smell. Some carrion-eating species, such as New World vultures and kiwis, are noteworthy exceptions.

Birds are very sensitive to touch, and many will roost together, bodies pressed close. But touch requires contact, and birds often communicate over a considerable distance.

Sound is a good means of communication at night or in other conditions of poor visibility. Owls, poor-wills, and other species are most often active at night and use vocalization to attract mates or establish territories. Small songbirds and other species may migrate at night, using simple calls to maintain contact with each other.

Sound is good for communicating around objects. The singing bird need not be in view for its general location to be known. It may be helpful if it cannot be precisely determined exactly where the sound originates, as when a bird utters an alarm note in the presence of a predator, alerting others to the predator's presence without betraying its explicit location to the hunter.

Sound presents information quickly. However, it has a high energy cost compared with some other means of communication. The laying down of scent, for example, may be somewhat incidental, as when a

The hauntingly beautiful call of the Hermit Thrush contains a blend of harmonics immensely pleasing to the human ear.

canine urinates both to relieve itself and to mark territory, and thus requires little extra energy expenditure. Appearance may be a passive means of communication. A male Scarlet Tanager in breeding plumage is bright red and need not expend extra energy to convey the identity of the species to female Scarlet Tanagers and to birders alike. On the other hand, an Eastern Kingbird has a concealed patch of red within the feathers of the crown. When attacking larger birds, the kingbird reveals the otherwise hidden red, thus slightly changing its appearance. Many breeding displays dramatically transform a bird's appearance at increased energy cost.

Birds communicate most frequently by sight and sound. Sound can communicate farther and in a broader range of circumstances than can a visual image. A sound is more specifically communicative than appearance, scent, or touch. It can be employed only as required. Thus, while sound production comes with a relatively high energy cost to the bird, the bird receives a high rate of return on the investment, in terms of conveying information.

This is not to say that a bird has the freedom or ability to produce any sound within its overall repertoire at any given time. The bird's ability and desire and the development of the physical part of the brain that controls the production of songs associated with breeding are governed by internal hormonal secretions, which, in turn, are triggered by such outside conditions as changes in length of daylight (photoperiodism) or the presence or absence of a reliable food source.

When Birds Sing

More songbirds sing more often and more completely at dawn than at any other time of day, with various species chiming in at different times. In the breeding season, in forested or semiforested areas, the dawn chorus can be impressive. It has been calculated that a song sung at dawn can be twenty times more effective than if performed at midday. This is believed by scientists to be primarily because climatic conditions at dawn are usually most favorable for sound transmission. At dawn there are less likely to be errant breezes, and perhaps there is less background noise (certainly true in urban areas at higher latitudes) than at most other times of day. For highly insectivorous species, the coolness of dawn may be less favorable for finding insects, so singing is better at midday, when insects are more active. As well, lower light levels impair the ability to find food in the early morning hours. Similarly, there is a lesser variant of the dawn chorus at dusk, when thrushes, particularly, can be heard to sing.

Birds sing or otherwise vocalize at other times, as well. The Red-eyed Vireo, one of temperate North America's most common birds, tends to sing all day long. American Robins are clearly dawn singers, but one can hear snatches of song, or even complete songs, at any time of the day.

Many songbirds will, at the height of the nesting season, sing at night, particularly if there is a full moon. I've received several complaints from people kept awake all night by a Northern Mockingbird outside the window. I can only reassure them that it is a phenomenon of short duration. Singing tends to decrease (except for brief snatches) as the moon wanes and as the breeding season advances.

Among nonsongbird species there are nocturnal species that most often will vocalize at night. Owls come first to mind, but members of the family Caprimulgidae, including such familiar North American species as Whip-poor-wills and Common Poor-wills, may also be quite nocturnal both in activity and in vocalization. Many aquatic species can be fairly active—and vocal—after dark. A marsh is often a fairly noisy place during the night, as moorhens and other species of rails, herons, and perhaps the odd duck vocalize to the accompaniment of frogs or the splash of a hunting mink or jumping fish. The Yellow Rail, a tiny marsh bird native to North America, is active during daylight but tends to give its breeding call at night. It is one of the most difficult birds to see, but in the right place, and at night, it is one of the easiest to hear.

Many migrant birds begin to develop their song during their migration and can be heard singing partial or full songs while still en route to their nesting grounds. Some species, such as the Northern Waterthrush, native to North America, will maintain small feeding territories on wintering grounds, and sometimes even during migration, although such territories often overlap and are not aggressively defended.

In the tropics, breeding, and hence maximum song production, may be more associated with dry or rainy seasons and with food supplies, whether or not such local conditions adhere to the calendar. Some species breed all year round.

Opportunistic breeding is prompted by favorable conditions, as opposed to seasonal change, and a well-known example of an oscine that practices opportunistic breeding is the Wattled Starling of central and southern Africa. The birds build nests in colonies, with large numbers of ball-shaped nests festooning shrubs or trees, sometimes placed so closely together as to merge. The Wattled Starling's urge to breed is triggered by outbreaks of locust swarms. As immense numbers of locusts pass like massive, clattering clouds over the African veldt, the birds quickly come into breeding condition. There will be plenty of food for hungry young Wattled Starlings. If the locust population collapses before the eggs are hatched or before the young are independent, the eggs or young will be abandoned. Singing may be accompanied by a visual display, both song and display serving to attract or maintain a mate.

In the North American Arctic and Subarctic, many species, such as the Snow Goose, may attempt nesting even though weather is inauspicious and food generally absent. In such circumstances, almost no young will survive.

Where Birds Sing

For audio communication to occur, the communicator must be heard. The farther away one is, the less of the sound produced reaches the ear, and objects, including vegetation, can alter, distort, absorb, or block sound. Therefore, many species will frequently sing from an elevated perch that allows the sound to travel, unimpeded, outward in all directions from the singer.

Thus a song perch is typically above surrounding vegetation, often out in the open. For suburban American Robins and European Starlings, TV antennas often served quite well as song perches, and now that antennas are less common, chimneys still provide rooftop song perches for urban birds. In the American Southwest, nonoscine species such as the Gambel's and California Quails also use such tall structures.

In the North American prairies, a low projection may allow enough elevation for species such as the Western Meadowlark, McCown's Longspur, or Lark Bunting. A stubby clump of cactus, a rock, a fence post, or a telephone wire may act as a song perch in open country. However, many field birds have also evolved flight songs, where the song "perch" is nothing less than the clear air above their territory. Such spectacular flight songs as those of the Bobolink, in North America, or the Skylark, of Europe, are well known. Snow Buntings have elaborate flight songs that are high-pitched, warbling, and musical as they tumble through the cool, clear air above northern tundra.

Because low-pitched, broad-frequency sounds carry better through vegetation, they are most often associated with birds that live deep in the forest, particularly terrestrial species. We will explore many examples later on, but often these sounds are described as "booming." One study of Neotropical birds showed that in the forest, bird songs tended to fall in the

The song of the Marsh Wren is particularly well suited to its habitat among the reeds and cattails of wetlands throughout much of North America.

1,600 to 25,000 Hertz range. Pure whistles were more prevalent in the forest than outside the forest. Work with European and North American songbirds has shown similar results.

Birds in marshes, where there is much more vegetation to absorb sound, tend, on average, to sing in lower frequencies than field birds, where the ground is surrounded by open air, not waving cattails and rushes. One of the deepest birds sounds, the "pump call" of that quintessential marsh bird, the American Bittern (which sounds like an old-fashioned farm water pump being primed), is very low-pitched and far carrying. Marsh and Sedge Wrens, native to North America, have higher-pitched calls but utter them from many different perches, as if trying to send them through the multitude of openings between cattails, tules, reeds, or sedges to compensate for the blockage of vegetation. Standing in the midst of a number of energetically singing Marsh Wrens, you can hear many songs from unseen singers, but inevitably some of the singers pop into your line of view and sing a song that arrives directly at your ears.

The Carolina Wren has shown an ability to match song to habitat. The species is found in a greater range of habitat than the Marsh Wren. Sounds were recorded from two different Carolina Wrens in two different habitats. Then each song was played in the other environment. What was discovered, through use of technical measurements, was that the songs transmitted with less degradation in the habitat where the bird sang than in the alternative habitat.

On the other hand, the Eurasian Chaffinch showed no song type differences among habitats. Nor, in North America, did American Redstarts. But some species in addition to the Carolina Wren do seem to use frequency ranges that are, to a measurable degree, reflective of the habitat of the singer. One internationally conducted study compared songs of Great Tits in Sweden, Norway, England, Spain, Iran, and Morocco. The conclusion was that the birds in forests utilized a narrower range of frequencies, had lower maximum frequencies, and utilized fewer notes than birds in drier, more open locations.

FOUR

A Few Features of Bird Sound

Songs

Most birds produce most sounds instinctively. Whether vocal or mechanical, the ability (and desire) to produce the sound is inherent. Certainly, for most songbirds, the vocalizations used in day-to-day activities, including those vocalizations associated with competition for a mate or for territory, are more or less part of the bird's instinctive repertoire. This does not necessarily mean that such birds do not benefit from hearing the sounds used, in appropriate contexts, by other members of their species. It simply means that the range of individual variation of the calls or other sounds is notably less among suboscines and most other birds than with regard to the songs of the oscines. There are exceptions, but with respect to both suboscines and nonpasserine species, learning plays less of a role, if any, in determining the sound produced than is true of the oscines' songs.

Calls

It is not always easy to try to classify something as dynamic as bird vocalization too rigidly. We seek such classification for our own ease of understanding, but the birds are under no obligation to assist us by neatly fitting their sounds into our classifications.

Calls tend to be short, simple, unrelated to breeding season, and uttered by both sexes. But the short "call" of the Henslow's Sparrow, barely more than a slurred click, seems to serve as a song, not a call, although the species also has a more complex flight song, rarely heard. On the other hand, the *chick-a-dee-dee-dee* of the Black-capped Chickadee, heard all year round, is actually a call. In breeding season, the male sings a sad, little two-note call that, to my ear, sounds like *sooo—saaddd*.

Most oscine songs consist of trills, or arrangements of notes, phrases, or trills. They are often complex, uttered by the male, and sometimes by the female, although often hers is either a different song or one that is sung in concert with the male's as a duet. They are used to establish territory and/or attract mates.

Contact Calls

Calls between members of a group of birds, either of the same species or mixed species, are called contact calls. They may keep the birds closer together in situations where visibility is hampered, perhaps because of darkness, fog, or thick foliage. Parent birds of many species use them to keep their chicks close by. Contact calls may help distract or confuse stalking predators by sounding first in one place, and then another. Contact calls are often heard among a flock of shorebirds, or other birds within close visual contact, and may serve some other function. Possibly for some species, it is a means of reassuring themselves that they are together and well, within a sometimes hostile world.

Alarm Calls and Warning Signals

Alarm calls serve to warn of a predator. Put very generally, such calls tend to cover a narrow frequency range, are more highly pitched than contact calls, and are of longer duration. A bird may give a loud warning call that serves to destroy the element of surprise for an approaching predator by alerting all nearby members of the flock or other birds (and sometimes other species) of the threat.

Mobbing Calls

Small birds may, upon discovering a predator, such as an owl, deliver a call that attracts other birds. The small birds swarm about the owl or hawk, calling constantly. The angry-sounding *caws* of a flock of American Crows swarming around a roosting owl are one of the better-known examples of noise associated with mobbing behavior. The function is to draw attention to the predator and to distract it, possibly to the point of driving it away. Mobbing calls of one species are often recognized as such by other species, which may join in harassing a common foe. Birders take advantage of this characteristic by uttering a "generic" mobbing call—usually a hissing or "pishing" or "sishing" sound, or a thin squeak—to attract local birds into view.

Distraction Behavior

Some birds, in the presence of a threat, use calls to draw attention to themselves and away from their eggs or young. As many an American schoolchild has seen firsthand, the Killdeer, which often nests on playgrounds, may act as though injured, while calling plaintively and moving away from cryptically colored eggs or chicks. This instinctive reaction to a perceived threat is similar to many such displays, silent or otherwise, by a variety of bird species, particularly ground-nesting ones. I have watched my two dogs follow what, to them, was an oddly acting and probably crippled Ruffed Grouse. She led the canines into the woods and away from her chicks. Once grouse and dogs were some distance from the chicks, the grouse suddenly "recovered." The dogs might have momentarily thought they were close to catching her, but she was never in danger. Except for her thrashing of leaves, the grouse, unlike the Killdeer performing in similar fashion, was silent.

Food Begging Calls

Consider a baby Blue Jay, an oscine common in much of eastern and midwestern North America. Early in life, jays develop a rather plaintive *wah* call. All baby Blue Jays have essentially the same call. It may increase in frequency of delivery as food approaches, and it may wax and wane in strength depending on the robustness of the bird's constitution or the degree of hunger. However, it is always essentially the same (allowing for minor individual variation) and is always identifiable as the noise made by a hungry baby Blue Jay.

I believe that the *wah* sound of the baby Blue Jay is such a powerful release, or trigger, inducing the parent bird to stuff food into the little bird's mouth, that it can work on other species. In fact, it works on me. I can't hear the sound, especially in conjunction with the visual aspects of the baby bird begging food, without wanting to feed the youngster.

The *wah* is uttered through a wide open mouth that has a thin, white line bordering it (the lip flanges) and a deep rose-pink color that darkens toward the center. Furthermore, the *wah* is usually accompanied by a small but effective suite of supplementary activities, including a shuffling or sidling forward, intensive wing-quivering (typical of baby songbirds begging for food) and possibly crouching, plus an increasing frequency of calls with a trace of a squeak suggesting great desperation.

Similar begging calls and behavior are common to all oscines and many nonoscine species. Female birds often imitate such behavior in pre-copulatory displays in front of males. Like a baby bird, they will crouch, flutter their wings, and beg for food. Some breeding displays involve a rit-ualistic placement of food by the male into the mouth of the female. Male terns regularly provide a fish to the female during mating rituals. Male pet Budgerigars, or budgies, will sometimes regurgitate seed to feed to the female. The urge may become so strong that in the absence of a mate, the budgie may try to feed his mirror image, or even his human companion

Call Variation in Songbirds
A colony-nesting songbird widely distributed in the Northern Hemi-sphere, the Bank Swallow (also known as the Sand Martin) feeds its babies in the nest for the first two weeks. The nest is one of many holes dug in the more or less perpendicular face of a sandy bluff or embankment. Finding the right hole to enter is certainly an achievement in spatial orientation. But after about the fifteenth day of life, the young swallows leave the nest cavity and join swarms of similarly aged and similarly appearing young swallows. Studies indicate that the parent birds can pick out their own young, based on the two-note food call of the newly fledged babies.

The same ability exists with the Cliff Swallow, a familiar North Amer-ican species that also nests in fairly dense colonies. On the other hand, the widely distributed Barn Swallow, which nests in shared habitats (often abandoned or little-used buildings) but not in dense colonies, does not seem to produce a chick with an individualistic food-specific call. At least some species of nonpasserine colony-nesting birds can also identify their own young by their calls.

Songs
A naturalist and sometimes poet, the Reverend Gilbert White (1720–93) was a meticulous observer of nature at his long-time residence in Sel-borne, Hampshire, England. At one point in his career, he realized that he had a bit of a mystery on his hands. A small bird, called at the time the Willow Wren, was quite common. Curiously, it seemed to sing three dif-ferent songs.

White began to keep track of which birds were singing which songs. He shot specimens of each song type and laid them out side by side to compare measurements, subtle variations in plumage color, and the coloring of their feet. It became clear that there was not just one species, but three, now known as the Wood Warbler, the Willow Warbler, and the Chiffchaff. The third, by the way, is named for its monotonous two-note song, uttered over and over again with so little variation as to seem as much a call as a song. It became apparent that there were other differences among these three similar species, such as nest construction and choice of habitat, but all such discovery started with White's close attention to the sounds the birds made.

Most songbird songs are at least a touch more varied than that of the Chiffchaff. Some are quite varied indeed. As a youngster, I owned a vinyl record by the late W.W.H. Gunn that featured various native songbirds—it was a pioneering birdsong recording. One of the birds on the record was the Magnolia Warbler. Many variations of the song were given. What impressed me was that while there was a similarity to each song, each was different, even though the many variations were given by the same bird. It was also frustrating. Not being gifted with an ear for subtle distinctions in birdsongs, how could I ever learn them if there was such variation within a single individual of a single species?

One author describes the Magnolia Warbler song as "a short, variable series of rich musical notes, often transcribed as *'weety weety wee'* or *'weety weety weety wee,'* with the last note sounding higher." Yes, that description is enough to evoke memories of spring woodlots with budding twigs bright in morning sunlight as northbound Magnolia Warblers hop about, flashing their white wing and tail patches, and singing *weety weety weety wee*, with the last note sometimes higher.

The songs of the Yellow Warbler are no less variable than those of the Magnolia—indeed, the Yellow Warbler has a much wider breeding distribution throughout North America and the tropics, with numerous races and regional variations in its song. However, there is, as is the case with the Magnolia, a basic species-specific structure to the Yellow Warbler's song, wherever it is heard. This is generally true of all oscines. Even the mimics tend to mimic in a species-specific manner.

There is, to oscine song, a basic pattern. In species with similar songs, that similarity may indicate a common origin, thus reflecting phylogeny—the evolutionary paths that led to the present species. But the basic structure is not enough. The bird may be hatched with a vocal outline or template in place, but to perfect the song, he must hear his father (or other singing males) and must practice. Each species of warbler is born with a template intact, and then learns refinement. In migrants of mid and high latitudes, the primary learning period typically is followed by a period of silence while the bird migrates or is on the wintering grounds. The song is then tested, and the process of perfecting it begins, usually on the wintering grounds.

Learning to Sing

The Common, or Island, Canary is native to the western Canary Islands, the Azores, and Madeira, off the northwest coast of Africa. There are about thirty-seven species in the genus *Serinus,* to which the canary belongs. On the following page I've illustrated some members of the genus that are native to Africa.

Canary breeders seeking to "improve" the song of the Common Canary have, for hundreds of canary generations, selected the "best" singers, as they subjectively judged quality of song.

But they discovered that it wasn't simply a matter of genetics, which did not, at any rate, exist as a science in the early decades of keeping captive canaries. In order to sing particularly well, as defined by the fancier, the bird had to be raised within hearing of other birds that sang well. The

Some African Canaries. Top, middle: *The Island Canary (*Serinus canaria*), native to the Azores, Madeira, and Canary Islands, is the progenitor of the domestic canary, renowned for its song.* Upper right: *The Serin (*S. serinus*) is found throughout much of Europe and North Africa, withdrawing from the northern part of its range in winter.* Mid-left: *The African Citril (*S. citrinelloides*) is restricted to East Africa.* Middle: *The Thick-billed Seedeater (*S. burtoni*) is a large, drab-colored canary with a distinctively heavy beak. It has a disjunct range through central Africa.* Mid-right: *The Black-eared Canary (*S. mennelli*) sometimes sings in gardens in its range in southern Africa, from southern Tanzania south through Zimbabwe to northern Mozambique.* Lower right: *The Streaky Seedeater (*S. striolatus*) is a robust canary found in the Sudan, Ethiopia, Tanzania, Kenya, and northern Zimbabwe. Its monotonous call usually consists of three high-pitched notes, blended and slurred upward at the end. Its song starts with a similar note but blends into a series of chips.* Lower left: *The Yellow-fronted Canary (*S. mozambicus*) is also known as the Green Singing Finch, the Yellow-breasted Canary, or the Yellow-eyed Canary. It is widely distributed throughout much of Africa, and its bright coloring and lovely voice make it a very popular cage bird.*

Barry Kent MacKay '97

better the teachers and the more intense the exposure to their singing, the better the pupil.

Song Development

Each songbird species appears to have a characteristic phase when it is receptive, or most receptive, to learning song. Some species, such as the Indigo Bunting, native to eastern North America, seem to be predisposed to learn better as young adults than as hatchlings and fledglings.

Zebra Finches, native to Australia and widely domesticated as an abundant cage bird species, become most receptive to learning songs at about thirty-five days of age, precisely the time they become independent of their parents. This period of receptivity lasts until the Zebra Finches are about sixty-five days of age. This does not mean that learning might not occur at other parts of a Zebra Finch's life, only that he is most likely to learn the songs of his species when he is between thirty-five and sixty-five days of age. When deprived of tutorial guidance during that critical period, the Zebra Finch will sing songs similar to those heard before (the songs of his father) or after that time period, as if to make do. The most developed and typical songs are learned during a few weeks after leaving parental care.

For White-crowned Sparrows, found as a breeding or wintering species in nearly all of North America, there are indications that peak learning occurs between approximately ten and fifty days of age. Social interaction, not just the ability to hear what is to be learned, may be crucial to learning.

A debate began with one study that, using tape recordings, demonstrated that the White-crowned Sparrow is, as one might expect, predisposed only to learn White-crowned Sparrow songs. However, another set of experiments, using live birds instead of recordings as audio role models, showed that White-crowned Sparrows that had physical access to live "tutors" of a different species would tend to learn the other species' song. Thus White-crowned Sparrows learned the songs of adult Song Sparrow tutors kept in the same enclosure. More surprising still, they even learned the song of a Red Avadavat, also called the Strawberry Finch.

Although they don't particularly sound alike, White-crowned Sparrows and Song Sparrows are both native to North America and reasonably closely related to each other. But the Red Avadavat is a tiny Asian species that is quite unlike either the White-crowned or the Song Sparrow in appearance and song, and is not at all closely related to either.

The Eurasian Chaffinch
In the 1950s, Dr. William H. Thorpe, in England, started raising chaffinches in isolation from their parents and any other audio role models. Others were raised in circumstances that allowed them to hear adults singing, as would be the case in the wild. By analyzing sonograms, Thorpe and other researchers were able to examine the vocalizations the birds produced.

The songs sung by the Eurasian Chaffinches raised in isolation from the sound of adult songs were certainly chaffinch songs, being about the right length and in the correct frequency range, and even structured similarly. And yet their quality was very poor. They were crude versions of the wild Eurasian Chaffinch's song, lacking the refinement and detail of the typical wild adult song.

A characteristic of the Eurasian Chaffinch's normal song is a flourish of cheerful notes at the end, very visible on a sonogram. This brief little upbeat conclusion to the song was named the *kit* by the German ornithologist who first made note of the feature. Many of Thorpe's chaffinches, raised in isolation from the sound of adult songs, lacked the distinctive *kit*.

Eurasian Chaffinches cease singing in August. The young chaffinches hatched that year will not, themselves, sing until the following spring. Thus their songs are separated from their learning by several months of silence.

Thorpe, and later other scientists, discovered that the Eurasian Chaffinches have two learning periods: The first is as hatchlings and fledglings, when they hear their own father and other local males singing. The following spring, Eurasian Chaffinches again become receptive, for part of that first breeding season, to learning and refining their songs.

However, after that, the windows of opportunity for the song-learning process apparently shut down for the rest of the birds' lives. Notwithstanding an inability to learn a new song, the Eurasian Chaffinch may continue to modify the songs of his existing repertoire, changing them slightly from season to season.

Other songbird species appear to have similar periods of receptivity to song learning. Indications are that if a songbird is deaf when young, he can never develop any more than a crude approximation of the song of his own species, as he lacks any means of learning the detail and intricacies of the full version. If, however, an adult songbird becomes deaf after having gone through the learning stage, he can still sing the full song. Only a small fraction of all songbird species have been as intensely studied as the Eurasian Chaffinch, and generalities may not hold true for every single kind of bird.

Distribution of Chaffinch Song Types

Eurasian Chaffinches are widely distributed through much of Europe, western Asia, northern Africa, and the Middle East. The Eurasian Chaffinch has been introduced into New Zealand, where it now thrives, as well as South Africa. It is also found on the Canary Islands. So is the very similar Blue Chaffinch, except that it is found *only* in high-elevation pine forests of the western Canary Islands.

In effect, the ancestor common to both the Eurasian and the Blue Chaffinch would have arrived in the Canary Islands long enough ago to evolve into the distinctive present species.

But then Eurasian Chaffinches again reached the Canary Islands, to meet up with the now specifically distinct Blue Chaffinches. That the color of the birds had changed is obvious, but what interests students of songbird song development is the manner in which the songs diverged from whatever they once were. We can only guess what the common ancestor of the Blue Chaffinch and the Eurasian Chaffinch sounded (or looked) like, but we can clearly determine how different they have become.

The Blue Chaffinch's song appears to have "deteriorated," if not from the song of the two species' common ancestor—a song we can never know—at least in comparison to the song sung by the contemporary Eurasian Chaffinch. The song of the Blue is slower, has just a few repeated notes, and has replaced the *kit* at the end of the song with several harsh notes.

Eurasian Chaffinch Regional Variation

Throughout its extensive range, the Eurasian Chaffinch has evolved into several subspecies. Its song occurs in a variety of regional dialects. All are identifiable as Eurasian Chaffinch songs in distinction from Blue Chaffinch songs, or songs of any other species.

A recent study of Eurasian Chaffinches in the Canary Islands was designed to see if their songs were more or less variable than those of mainland birds. Looking at the most basic single song elements, no significant difference was noted. With regard to the more complex song elements, the Canary Island Eurasian Chaffinches were found to have significantly greater variation than Eurasian Chaffinch songs in Iberia.

The song of the Blue Chaffinch, found only on the Canary Islands,
has deteriorated in complexity when compared to mainland relatives.

A tentative conclusion was that the island birds had, in effect, greater room for variability, as there was essentially a much smaller population, thus less competition among singing males, than on the mainland. A comparison might be made from sports or business. In a field of three, a poor runner may fare much better than in a field of ten. A bread company may have better luck marketing an inferior brand of bread in a market with only two other competitors than in a market where the consumer has seven brands to choose from. Thus reduced competition on the island may result in less demand toward the degree of refinement to be found on the mainland.

Eurasian Chaffinches in New Zealand

While it was not the intent, introducing Eurasian Chaffinches to New Zealand allowed scientists to observe firsthand the very basic stages of song evolution as they occur when a founder population becomes isolated from the main stock.

Not only have the New Zealand chaffinches changed their songs slightly, those on the North Island of New Zealand have a "dialect" subtly distinct from those on the South Island. That fact provided scientists with an idea to try a simple experiment. Chaffinches were moved from North Island to South Island, where they were caged for study. Thirty males were involved. They were moved only 380 kilometers. Either before or just after capture, their songs were carefully recorded so that subsequent changes could be detected.

After the transferred birds were released, three of them were found the following spring. They were still singing with their North Island "accents." However, two of the birds had modified their contact calls to resemble those of the South Island birds who were their new neighbors. Thus, while we think of calls as "instinctive" compared to song, they may, in fact, be units of vocalization that can, under appropriate influence, change. At least, that is true of the Eurasian Chaffinch. The ability would appear to have a selective advantage (that is to say, an advantage that would be passed on to the next generation) as the two birds with the new, southern contact calls were mated. The third bird, retaining his northern call, was not mated.

With regard to chaffinches, it was tentatively concluded that the nature of the songs was not as important in attracting mates (although presumably it was still paramount in declaring and defending territory against rival males) as was the nature of the contact calls.

We don't know why changes occurred. Those sounds that work best in one environmental context may be less successful in a new situation. Thus, on average and over time, the old ones are selected against, either because they have a negative impact on a bird's ability to survive (albeit in some way we do not understand) or because they don't work as well within such social contexts to attract a mate—also for reasons we do not understand.

The Oscine's Template for Song Learning

During those critical windows of opportunity when the young male songbirds are most likely to learn the refinements of the song of their species, why do they not learn the wrong song, as there are singing males of other species sharing their habitats?

Sometimes they do learn the wrong song, but it appears that generally the young bird, when receptive to song learning, also instinctively filters out the "wrong" songs, particularly when the "right" songs are being heard. This supports evidence of an inherited, species-specific template. The fact that a White-crowned Sparrow can learn a Red Avadavat's song indicates that in the absence of the song of his own species, the young male may give in to something quite different from the structure of the template. But in general, when the young White-crowned Sparrow, in learning mode, hears the songs of the Blackpoll Warbler, Common Redpoll, Lincoln's Sparrow, Rusty Blackbird, or other neighbors, he filters them out in favor of the sounds of his father and other White-crowned Sparrows.

Isolating Factors

Recently, concerns emerged from Britain that young songbirds were failing to adequately develop the songs of their species in areas where background traffic noises interfered with the ability of the young birds to adequately hear their respective role models. Males with inadequate songs may not be able to compete with males with fully developed songs, either to maintain territories or to attract mates.

Songs, habitat preferences, appearances, and visual displays all serve to genetically isolate species by keeping them breeding within their own species. Each species evolves in occupation of an ecological niche consisting of other animals and plants, also evolving. Through long periods of evolution, they all tend to accommodate each other in a dynamic, ever-changing world. Hybridization can produce a mixture of characteristics that do not "fit in" to the ecological niche of either parent, or at least not well enough to allow the hybrid an equal opportunity to survive.

The subtle regional differences in call notes may be a determining factor in mate selection, and may not be entirely fixed and inflexible. The features that distinguish one species from another can evolve only if such isolating mechanisms are at work. Song—sometimes including songs or calls in conjunction with visual display—is, for most species, a major isolating mechanism serving to keep closely related species from interbreeding.

In the lower Great Lakes region of North America, the ranges of two closely related songbird species, the Blue-winged Warbler and the Golden-winged Warbler, overlap. The two species sometimes interbreed, producing viable offspring. Blue-wings are extending their ranges north into what historically was the range of the Golden-winged. The two species have very similar songs and sometimes sing the same song. Obviously, filters and templates are not sufficiently developed from each other to prevent the two species from interbreeding.

The Blue-winged and Golden-winged Warblers have a relatively recent common ancestor. We can assume that the original isolating factor that separated populations of that ancestor was a climatic or geographic barrier, presumably during the ice ages. Unlike the two chaffinch species, the two warbler species did not evolve far enough to develop completely successful isolating mechanisms.

Female Song

For most species of songbirds, both sexes have a variety of calls, but it's usually the male who does most or all of the singing. In many tropical species, the female will sing with the male, in duet. But does the female sing independently? Not usually, although there are many exceptions. The hormone testosterone produces in the male bird the urge to sing. Testosterone in the female can also stimulate song.

The part of the brain that controls song is bigger and more complex in the male than in the female bird. However, it has been shown that the female songbird's brain can change to more resemble that of the male, with regard to the part that controls song, in response to artificially induced higher levels of testosterone. Testosterone not only urges singing, it also triggers the physiological changes that make singing possible.

A study involving Willow Tits, a Eurasian species very similar to North America's chickadees, showed that testosterone levels in wild males increased at the time the birds began to sing. Testosterone levels in females showed no such increase. However, there was a slight increase in female testosterone levels in August, which corresponded with when female Willow Tits may tend to do some singing.

European Robin
The European Robin sings boisterously year-round. Males show an increase in testosterone in the breeding season, as expected, and change their behavior accordingly, becoming territorial and aggressive toward rival males or anything remotely like a rival male, even going so far as to attack a ball of cotton stained a robin-breast red. Females have no such increase in testosterone levels. In winter, both sexes are somewhat territorial, each defending his or her own feeding territory—with song.

It appears, therefore, that the European Robin's song production is not as dependent upon testosterone levels as is true of other species that have been studied. The European Robin has a large repertoire of song types to choose from and varies the sequence in which they are given. Notwithstanding the European Robin's well-known tenacity in attacking objects of similar size and color, the species is more discerning when it comes to audio recognition. Studies indicate that the European Robin recognizes neighbors' songs and can distinguish the song of a newcomer to the neighborhood. A newcomer is more likely to be attacked. Other songbird species have shown similar ability.

Visual cues are also important to the European Robin. As Rosemary Jellis wrote in her excellent book, *Bird Sounds and Their Meaning* (Cornell University Press, 1977): "In situations [of conflicts between male birds] . . . visual information is particularly important. Stylized movements may enhance the eye-catching effect of part of the plumage as, for instance, when a [European] Robin engaged in threatening a rival puffs out the red throat and breast to maximum size. But movements may be supplemented by sound. If the rival fails to wilt at the sight of that rich expanse of red feathers, the [European] robin often makes doubly sure, according to the intensity of the threat, or its own mood at the moment, by singing a terse, strangulated phrase quite unlike the normal fluent sound."

In North America, one study found that out of 140 wild Song Sparrow females, 12 produced song. One literature review found no less than 40 songbird species in which the female was known to sing. As more work is done, particularly in tropical regions, that figure will undoubtedly increase.

Red-winged Blackbirds and Female Songs

Red-winged Blackbirds are abundant throughout most of North America, are conspicuous, and tend to nest together in loosely formed colonies, usually in cattail marshes. They have evolved into regional races and have several near relatives.

Red-winged Blackbirds are polygynous, meaning each male may have several mates. The males will sit on the top of a cattail, or on an overhead branch or possibly a telephone wire, and sing their distinctive, if not particularly musical, songs. The song is accompanied to a varying degree by a visual display that utilizes the brilliant red lesser wing coverts. When the male Red-wing displays at his most intense level, he contorts himself, tail twisted downward, wings partly or fully spread, and red epaulets fluffed to their fullest extent, and gives his distinctive song, a gurgling jumble of notes followed by a longer, discordant call. This is called the spread song.

Female Red-winged Blackbirds, of a modest, streaked pattern, also sing throughout the breeding season. Their songs are different from those of the males, and some research indicates two distinct female song types. One song is a personal response from the female to her mate. It is rather as if the female were reminding the male that however many mates he may have, she is one of them. The second sound type is directed toward a rival female. Each female maintains a small nesting territory from which other females, even if mated to the same male, are excluded.

Whisper Song

A whisper song, also widely known as a subsong, is a minor variation of a full song. The subsong tends to be a prolonged, rambling series of vocalizations that are not employed to attract mates or proclaim territory, are not necessarily seasonal, and are sung at such low volume that they can be heard only a short distance away.

I heard a great deal of subsong from a Painted Redstart that lived with my family for many years. The little bird, the first of his kind ever to be found in Canada, had been rescued in southern Ontario just prior to the onslaught of winter. As he was a subtropical species, release back into the wild would have been fatal. Because she specialized in the care of small, avian insectivores, my mother received the bird for safekeeping.

The little bird never became fully tame, but neither was he fully wild. He would sing, in season, a song that fit the books' descriptions of what a Painted Redstart should sound like. But he also engaged, as did many other songbirds in our care, in whisper singing, or subsong. This subsong consisted of a steady stream of notes and phrases, including those that seemed to be low-volume versions of the actual territorial song. The sub-song was invariably sung only when the bird appeared to be completely content. He would fluff the feathers of his flanks, and either perched on one foot or sitting flat, he quietly sang. His eyes seemed to be partly shut, and his head was very slightly tilted back. His throat would puff in and out, and sometimes he'd look around as he sang. This whisper singing would happen only when all was calm and quiet. He did not mind familiar humans in the room so long as we were not moving about. He did not mind sound so long as it was a monotonous and familiar back-ground sound, such as a radio or television or quiet human conversation. Any change or disturbance would cause him to become instantly alert. Otherwise, when he was finished with his subsong, or during a pause, he would often stretch high on both legs or spread his wings, much like a human rousing from a brief bit of daydreaming. Then, perhaps, he would fly over to take nourishment or water from small dishes we pro-vided, and then either fly about the room looking for the fruitflies, root maggot flies, and mealworms we provided for him to find as he hunted, or return to his subsong.

My concerns about anthropomorphism notwithstanding, that bird gave every indication that he was singing entirely to himself as a function of being very comfortable, relaxed, and feeling secure. Every subsong I've heard has given me that same perception of a bird experiencing content-ment. There are, however, references to subsong being a response to stress. Perhaps it is thereby employed as a "displacement activity"—an activity that results from conflict or emotion but has no practical function, rather like head-scratching by a puzzled human.

I have heard the same type of subsong under the same kinds of cir-cumstances from other captive songbirds, particularly among the various thrush species. However, that form of singing is likely different from the softly uttered contact vocalizations between two individuals of the same species. Such subsong may be associated with behavior that is anything but relaxed, or at least, one observer so notes when applying the term to vocalization of the Great Tit that is directed toward another bird, accom-panied by rapid wing fluttering.

I think that what I've described for the Painted Redstart, and heard from various songbird species, comes closer to what seems to be a type of practicing, called a subsong, that has been described for Nightingales. For that Eurasian thrush species, the act of voicing a subsong starts at about six months of age. The subsong seems to build toward the complete song through time, becoming the full song by commencement of the breeding season, in the spring. Adult male Nightingales sing the full song for about four weeks.

Within the stream of utterances that constitute the Nightingale's subsong are those phrases that, with some fine-tuning, will constitute the full song. These are called identified patterns, or IPAs. The IPAs are in distinction to those parts of the flow of sound that are not part of the final song and are called unidentified patterns, or UPAs. Just as there are notes that a musician puts together, so are there such basic units to a songbird's song.

Mimicry

Hill Mynahs, native to southern Asia, are widely familiar as cage birds. Their popularity is primarily a result of the species' uncanny ability to mimic the human voice.

It might be assumed that the Hill Mynah is a superb mimic of other birds in the wild. Such is not the case. In the wild, the Hill Mynahs learn from others of their own kind, but what they learn is refinement on whoops and calls, and neither the structured sound of, say, a chaffinch nor the endlessly variable mimicry of a European Starling or a Northern Mockingbird. In captivity, the constant repetition of sounds, including the human voice, provides something for the mynah to learn. In the wild, it seems that the species *must* be exposed to species-specific calls in order to learn them well enough to use them. Not only that, but the learning is also gender-specific, with male mynahs learning male calls and females learning female calls.

In the wild, the Hill Mynah utters a loud call. It does not resemble what human listeners might consider to be a song. These calls come in a variety of types, and they seem to serve the purpose of mate attraction and bonding that is to be found in more typical songbird songs. Territoriality is probably less of a biological concern to the Hill Mynah than to many other songbird species, because mynahs tend to be rather gregarious during nesting season. Their protection of territory may be more of a group

Top: *The Hill Mynah, noted in the wild for its loud cries and regional dialects, can be taught to quite accurately imitate the human voice.* Bottom: *The European (Common) Starling is in the same family as the mynahs, and like them, can imitate human words.*

defense than as protection from others of the same species. The plasticity of the call appears to allow the formation of "matched" calling between members of a mated pair, at least in some instances.

Minor "dialect" or "accent" variations in call types have been noted in groups of Hill Mynahs no more than 14 kilometers apart, although all calls are clearly those of Hill Mynahs. This suggests that, as is true of accents in human language, the birds form regional associations in which minor variations of pronunciation reinforce themselves in the absence of significant influence from birds with other accents.

Hill Mynahs are one of many species of birds noted for remarkable abilities at imitating other sounds. The fact that they may imitate sounds that are not a part of their natural environment, such as the sound of a human voice, further demonstrates that they can learn new vocalizations. Studies indicate that in terms of vocalizations serving biological functions in the wild, they *must* learn. Thus it would be incorrect to assign all of their vocal range to instinct.

One does not hear wild songbirds imitate the human voice. However, species like the European Starling, Northern Mockingbird, and Superb Lyrebird not only incorporate other bird species' songs into their own long, rambling serenades, but also mimic such things as human whistles, creaking hinges, barking dogs, and other human-related sounds from their aural environments. Blue Jays have a call that is similar to that of Red-tailed Hawks. Whether or not this derives from true mimicry, the cry so closely resembles that of the raptor that some birders do not assume that a hawk's call actually comes from a hawk until they see the hawk make the call. The Tufted, or Dickey's, Jay, endemic to a small region of Mexico, includes some mimicry in his song. So does the beautifully colored Green Jay of Mexico, northern Central America, and South America, a species particularly noteworthy for the variety of not particularly musical notes uttered in its rambling song.

Songbirds able to imitate the human voice include the widely distributed European Starling, and the American Crow and several of its relatives. The starling's imitation tends to be squeaky, and sometimes the "words" are apparent only to those familiar with the bird, but crows may speak human words with almost the same fidelity for which the mynah is so famous.

The Northern Mockingbird of North America and the Superb Lyrebird of Australia are famous as mimics with great fidelity to the sounds they

The Blue Jay, native to North America, has a call that resembles that of the Red-tailed Hawk.

copy. Up to about 70 percent of the lyrebird's song consists of mimicry of sounds from nonlyrebird sources.

A German researcher reported a charming little tale of Crested Larks learning a shepherd's whistle so well that the birds were able to fool the man's trained dogs into following certain whistled commands. Both Eurasian Jays and their close relatives from the Himalayas, the Lanceolated Jays, have been heard imitating dogs' barks. No doubt there are still other members of the jay, crow, raven, rook, chough, and magpie family, Corvidae, that practice varying degrees of mimicry.

Parrots

The most famous and accomplished of human voice mimics are found among a nonsongbird group, the parrots. Matched, if at all, only by the Hill Mynah as a human voice mimic is the African Gray Parrot. Many other parrots have this ability to greater or lesser degrees.

This wondrous talent for mimicry is all the more amazing by virtue of their being part of a family of birds for which words like "squawk" or "screech" or "chatter" seem custom made. Although some parrots, like the Scarlet-chested, or Splendid, Parakeet of Australia, give voice to no more than soft twittering, most parrots engage in loud chatter, squeaks, piping, trills, rattles, and yelps.

The cacophonous screeching of a flock of parrots may sound random and raucous, but careful study by field ornithologists demonstrates that— no less than other birds—parrots possess a vocabulary of predetermined vocalizations. Those vocalizations stimulate specific responses or communicate particular information, at least within the species. Contact calls, begging calls, mating calls, warnings—parrots do communicate such things among themselves. It also appears that there is greater plasticity, or range, in vocal options than is found among most other nonpasserine species.

Several parrot species engage in duets, with two, or possibly more, birds taking part in a single prolonged vocalization. Duet singing is believed to function primarily to strengthen pair bonding. The Monk Parakeet, of South America, frequently nests in large communal nests. Most of the birds in the colony may share a single contact call, uttered constantly.

Mimicry is most certainly not confined either to captive birds or to imitation of the human voice. Both the African Gray Parrot and at least some of the *Amazona* species of the Americas copy the calls of entirely different bird species. The African Gray has even been found imitating the call of a bat. It is possible that these "borrowed" calls enter the mating repertoire of the African Gray somewhat as imitated calls fill the songs of the mockingbird or the starling.

Bird Mimicry and Language

A couple decades ago, Irene Pepperberg, an American scientist, began some interesting and now famous work with an African Gray Parrot named Alex. Pepperberg was well aware that the common belief among scientists (although not necessarily experienced parrot owners) was that parrot mimicry was exactly that: a mechanically accurate but mentally irrelevant imitation of a sound heard. That sound might be a cat meowing, a door closing, or a human word, but it was uttered without reference to meaning.

Pepperberg approached Alex not just as a pet or companion, but as a research subject, and initiated a series of fascinating experiments. She first determined that although parrots are very different from songbirds, in the wild they have a songbirdlike need to imitate the adults and older role models of their own kind.

Any animal trainer will tell

In 1976, Richard Dawkins, in the interest of helping quantify the changes that occur in birdsong from bird to bird, generation to generation, coined the word *meme* to describe a unit of information that can be transmitted from one bird's brain to another's. This unit of learning, when applied to birdsong, becomes a song meme, or song pattern, that one bird utters and another bird learns. A meme may be a note or a single phrase. It may also be a block of audio elements within the larger context of a complete song, or even an entire song.

When scientists examine how song or song elements are transmitted, they look at the transferral of memes whose size (duration or complexity) may well be unique to a given species. Memes may occur within a bird or may vanish, and the rate at which this can happen is also a matter of study. ■

you that the key to training is the reward, most specifically food, doled out when the animal, from mouse to orca (and not excluding people), does the thing that is required. Intellect need play a small role in such training. Pepperberg changed this training method to providing "referential rewards." Alex would not be rewarded for talking; he would have to say the word that represented the thing he wanted. Thus he would have to say "nut" in order to be rewarded with a nut. If he said "spoon," he'd be given a spoon, not a nut.

Pepperberg used the same process to teach Alex basic colors. The parrot also learned associations between specific human words and the shapes those words represented. Thus they came to represent to him what they also would represent to a human child in the process of learning language.

I believe that if Alex had done no more than learn some basic nouns and use them referentially it would have been quite wonderful. That he learned descriptive adjectives and could apply them with high degrees of accuracy is still more remarkable. But he and Pepperberg went further. Alex learned self-expression. He learned to use the word "want" in a context that was appropriate to the circumstances. He learned to say "no" when he didn't "want" something. He learned to judge when two objects were the "same" and when they were "different." That is a skill that requires far more judgment than remembering the correct name of a color and applying that name accurately.

Alex and other parrots have demonstrated certain abilities by using human words in what appears to be a basic and identifiable grammar that, in a human, would be considered at least a precursor to language.

FIVE

Regional Variation and Speciation

Speciation refers to the evolution of distinct species. Species evolve when a population becomes divided. Isolation can be either physical or behavioral. When isolated, two or more populations may diverge—go their separate ways in terms of changing from their original forms—to the point where they may be considered separate species, unlikely to interbreed. The determination of when speciation has occurred is not always a simple matter; the "rules" are designed to facilitate understanding and discussion, but we must remember that the process of evolution is ongoing and dynamic and was never meant to fit into a rigid set of definitions.

Appearance is an obvious behavioral isolating mechanism. An Indigo Bunting does not look too much like a Lazuli Bunting. The two forms may interbreed in those few areas of North America where their breeding ranges overlap, suggesting that they are still races of the same species, but they do not do so randomly, suggesting that they are well on the way to becoming separate species and might be so regarded. Both the distinctive color differences and the different songs are obvious isolating mechanisms when the two species encounter each other. In the absence of such effective isolating mechanisms, the two forms will randomly interbreed, mixing various characters, until distinctiveness is lost.

Why does it matter? Put simply, the changes that occur are *adaptations*. Some are obvious—a longer wing, for example, may better serve birds in populations that migrate farther. But these adaptations may drift so far apart that hybrids are at a significant disadvantage compared with the offspring of true-breeding pairs. Obviously, whatever keeps birds breeding true will therefore serve to isolate those birds from their close relatives. Through time, this process is self-reinforcing.

Both professional ornithologists and casual birders need to be aware of the potential importance of vocalizations in determining different bird species. Physical characteristics, such as shape of body parts, measurements, color, and pattern, have traditionally been used to determine a species or subspecies of bird. Early naturalists could preserve and compare many such features. Prior to the development of sound recording and related technology, however, there was relatively little ability to preserve and objectively compare bird sounds. Birds depend on sound, in some cases exclusively, as a means of species identification.

Most beginning birders quite naturally first learn to identify birds by their appearance, but the skilled birder often uses sound, more than sight, to identify songbirds and other bird species in the field. Some species can be identified only by their sounds.

Empidonax Flycatchers

Older bird books featuring birds of North America mention a widely distributed, easily overlooked little bird called the Traill's Flycatcher. The bird's breeding range extended from Alaska to Newfoundland, south as far as New Mexico and Tennessee. Sharp-eared birders noticed that Traill's Flycatchers gave two types of songs. There were also two similar but distinct calls. In some areas, both songs and calls could be heard. To the north, however, only one sound, usually rendered *fee-beeo*, was uttered during the nesting season. To the south and in the western United States, the song was *fitz-bew*, rendered with sneezelike emphasis. During the spring migration, one might hear northward migrants utter either song.

More attention was paid to these two groups of birds in an effort to determine why they should have two distinct sets of vocalizations. It had been known since the 1950s that there were minor physical differences within the "species," and it was thought they probably represented an eastern and a western subspecies. When specimens of Traill's Flycatchers of known vocalization were examined very carefully, with multiple measurements taken and extremely close attention paid to the most minor details of color and pattern, it was discovered that the minor differences held true in relation to the vocalizations.

Although there was an area of overlap in the northeastern United States and southeastern Canada, extending west to the Caribou Parklands of central British Columbia, each of the two species had its own breeding range and, generally speaking, its own habitat preference (although with considerable overlap, both favoring marshier habitat, while the very similar Western Flycatcher favored more upland environs), plus minor but consistent variations in nest structure and location. The young of each of the two groups was more distinctive than the adults. It was therefore concluded that two distinct if very similar species existed.

In actuality the Traill's was two species, now known as the Willow Flycatcher *(Empidonax traillii),* given the original scientific name, as it was the form on which the description of the Traill's Flycatcher was first based, and the Alder Flycatcher *(E. alnorum).* When the birds are not calling, they cannot reliably be identified as to species and are collectively known as *Empidonax* flycatchers (usually pronounced em-PIH-don-ax).

The *fitz-bew* of the Willow is distinctly sneezelike, while the Alder's *fee-beeo* is less enthusiastic—a little more "buzzy" and laid back. The call of the Willow is a softer, more liquid *wit;* that of the Alder is a loud *preep* or, on the breeding grounds, a huskier *wheer.*

There are several other, similar *Empidonax* flycatchers whose ranges overlap in North America, but they can be distinguished not only by sound but, under good viewing conditions, by minor differences in appearance as well.

Western Flycatchers

The story of another *Empidonax,* the Western Flycatcher, is somewhat different. The Western Flycatcher *(E. difficilis)* breeds from southern British Columbia south through much of the western United States into northern Mexico. Field ornithologists had long noted that there were two distinct forms of the Western Flycatcher, identified as separate subspecies, each with a particular song and each with minor but distinctive differences in appearance. Upon further investigation, it was determined that the two races should have full species status. The Western Flycatcher was split into the Pacific Slope Flycatcher, given the original scientific name, *E. difficilis,* and the Cordilleran Flycatcher, *E. occidentalis.* As their names imply, Pacific Slope Flycatchers breed to the west of the Great Divide, while the Cordilleran Flycatcher breeds in the interior, through the Rockies, east of the Sierras.

The song, or call, of the Pacific Slope Flycatcher is a single, upslurred *tseeep,* sometimes interspersed with a sharp little *tik* note; the equivalent call of the Cordilleran Flycatcher has two notes, the first blending into the second, higher note.

Scientists carefully compared all features of these two groups. There was a problem. Unlike the Alder and Willow Flycatchers, the Pacific Slope and Cordilleran Flycatchers did interbreed, and they sometimes sang each other's songs. So while they were, for a while, split into separate species, they are now again generally considered to be two races of the same species, the Western Flycatcher. They have evolved from common ancestry, but not so far as to warrant, in the opinions of most ornithologists, full species status.

Other *Empidonax* Flycatchers

There are still more species of *Empidonax* flycatchers in North, Central, and South America. Some species have a reasonably distinctive appearance and can often be identified by sight alone. In some instances, there are no other similar flycatchers living within their ranges. But generally speaking, the genus presents classic examples of how variations in vocalizations, often rather minor to our ears, serve as isolating mechanisms among physically similar species. What is subtle to the human ear is distinctive when objective comparisons of spectrographs can be made, and no doubt highly distinctive to the birds themselves.

Hybrids among various *Empidonax* species have occurred, although finding hybrids between such similar species would be so difficult to accomplish that the small number recorded may not mean too much in terms of how often such hybridization actually occurs. However, if hybridization were random, the different forms would ultimately blend into one, a process called genetic swamping. The fact that this has not happened demonstrates that the birds are aware of who is whom. Their distinctive vocalizations allow them to recognize their own species.

West Indian Flycatchers

There are other genera of tyrant flycatchers consisting of several species that are physically similar to each other. One such genus is *Myiarchus*. In North America, the Great Crested Flycatcher is quite similar to the Brown-crested Flycatcher, while a sharp eye is required to tell an Ash-throated Flycatcher from a Dusky-capped Flycatcher. However, each species is still relatively distinctive in appearance, and each species has a very distinctive call.

The situation with some West Indian tyrant flycatchers is rather different. On each of many different islands in the West Indies could be found *Myiarchus* flycatchers that were pretty much alike in appearance. The isolation imposed upon them by being confined to different islands, as the species are not migratory and are not likely to cross wide stretches of the Caribbean Sea, led to some divergence. The birds tended to change in minor degrees of detail in appearance as they evolved from their common ancestor in isolation from each other.

Originally scientists lumped all the similar birds found in the Bahamas, Greater Antilles east to St. John, and Martinique as races of a single species, the Stolid Flycatcher. Then, in order to map the species and distribution of *Myiarchus* flycatchers in the West Indies, scientists decided to use recordings of their calls to find out what birds, on what islands, would respond to what calls. If Stolid Flycatchers from the Bahamas were challenged by recordings of calls from Cuban Stolid Flycatchers, or vice versa, but ignored calls from Jamaican Stolid Flycatchers—which, in fact, was the case—then clearly at least one isolating mechanism, the voice, had diverged to a sufficient degree to generally prevent hybridization.

As a result of this work, a group of forms originally lumped as one species, the Stolid Flycatcher, was split into four distinct species, each with its own song type. Cuban and Bahamian Stolid Flycatchers recognized each other's songs as their own and were renamed the La Sagra's Flycatcher *(Myiarchus sagrae).* The birds of Jamaica and Hispaniola and nearby islands retained the name Stolid Flycatcher *(M. stolidus).* The birds of Puerto Rico and the nearest Virgin Islands were named the Puerto Rican Flycatcher *(M. antillarum),* and the birds of the southern Lesser Antilles (Barbuda, St. Christopher, Nevis, Dominica, Martinique, and St. Lucia) were named the Lesser Antillean Flycatcher *(M. oberi).*

Although there were differences in appearance, these alone did not reveal that the Stolid Flycatcher of St. Thomas Island was specifically distinct from very similar Stolid Flycatchers from nearby Barbuda Island (which have less yellow below and less distinct wingbars than St. Thomas birds) and that both were different from similar birds found in Cuba and the Bahamas (flatter-headed, different posture, and slight color differences), and also distinct from similar birds found on Hispaniola or Jamaica (distinctly crested, yellowish belly, distinct wingbars, and light edges to flight feathers). It was vocalization that revealed that fact.

Other tyrant flycatcher species were also split on the basis of field studies that demonstrated reactions to voices of similar birds from different islands. What were formerly considered to be two resident species of pewees, members of the genus *Contopus,* were split into six distinct species. Originally the pewees that bred in the northern Bahamas, Cuba, Jamaica, Hispaniola, and Gonave Island were called the Greater Antillean Pewee *(C. caribaeus)* and the more warmly colored birds of the Lesser Antilles were called the Lesser Antillean Pewee *(C. latirostris).* Scientists noted minor, geography-specific color and measurement variations within each species, but did not conclude that such variations warranted species status.

In part due to the use of recordings to determine whether the birds did or did not respond to similar forms from other islands, there were profound changes in the classification of species. The name Crescent-eyed Pewee *(C. caribaeus)* was reserved for the form found on Cuba and in the northern Bahamas. It has a distinct, crescent-shaped white mark bracketing the back part of the eye. Birds from Hispaniola were determined to be a separate species, the Hispaniolan Pewee *(C. hispaniolensis).* The form restricted to Jamaica became the Jamaican Pewee *(C. pallidus).* The one found in Puerto Rico, where it is common, became the Puerto Rican Pewee *(C. portoricensis).* The name Lesser Antillean Pewee *(C. latirostris)* was retained only for the birds restricted to Guadeloupe, Dominica, Martinique, and possibly St. Christopher, where it has sporadically been reported. The pewees restricted to the island of St. Lucia, where they are common, were renamed the St. Lucia Pewee *(C. oberi).*

The fact that minor physical variations had evolved in forms found on one island or group of islands was rather useless in determining specific status, particularly if such forms were physically isolated. The species-determining question was whether or not the birds would interbreed. Scientists could easily move the recorded songs of the birds from place to place to see if they elicited breeding responses. Lack of such responses demonstrated that the song was an effective isolating mechanism, and thus specific status could be conferred. If the song elicited a breeding response, then even though the two populations might be physically separated and have differences in appearance, they had not yet evolved into distinct species. The same tests were done with other West Indian flycatchers. For example, it was determined that what has been called the Dusky-capped Flycatcher *(Myiarchus tuberculifer)* in Jamaica was a species distinct from the Dusky-capped Flycatcher found on the mainland, from southeastern Arizona south deep into South America. The Jamaican bird was renamed the Sad Flycatcher *(M. barbirostris).*

Similarly, the Grenada Flycatcher *(M. nugator)* was formerly considered to be a race of the mainland Brown-crested, or Rusty-tailed,

Flycatcher *(M. tyrannulus),* which is found from the southern United States south into South America.

Eastern and Western Meadowlarks

There is no sound sweeter and more evocative of the open plains and dry, yucca-studded uplands of western North America than the song of the Western Meadowlark. Not at all a lark, this oscine, a member of the family Icteridae, has a mottled brown back, wings, and tail; brown and white striping on the head; a yellow throat and breast; and a distinctive black crescent across the upper chest. The outer tail feathers are white and show prominently as the bird flies away.

That same description also fits a different species, the Eastern Meadowlark, native to eastern North America. Its breeding range extends south through Mexico, into southern Central America and northern South America, including Colombia, Venezuela, the Guianas, and northern Brazil, reaching lower Amazonia. There is also a breeding population in Cuba.

There are minor but consistent differences in pattern and color between the two meadowlark species. These are among a set of subtle distinctions in color and pattern that are of little value to birders in telling the two species apart in the field. What keeps these birds from randomly breeding where their breeding ranges overlap? Song appears to be the single most significant isolating mechanism, with differences great enough to prevent confusion among either birders or birds. The songs of the two species are very distinctive.

The Western Meadowlark's song starts with a little assembly of notes that blend into an enthusiastic and accelerating gurgling or bubbling sound, typically ending on a high note. The Eastern Meadowlark's full song is usually a double, triple, or quadruple note, a slightly melancholy slurred whistle—*see-you, see-yer* or *pee-you, pee-yay* or, as I wrote as a youngster, *wheet-tee-year, wheet-to-you* or *slow-UP, slow down.*

Eastern Meadowlarks show tremendous variations of songs based on the basic, species-specific theme. These variations in song types sung by a single bird are referred to as that bird's repertoire. Eastern Meadowlarks have large repertoires, fifty-five found in one study. Western Meadowlarks have relatively modest repertoires; three to twelve different songs may be sung by one bird in one season, with about eight probably being typical.

The two species of birds obviously derive from a common ancestor. Divergence of an identifying character—in this case vocalization—is

Barry Kent MacKay

required to assist genetic integrity. The less they sound alike, the less likely the two species will interbreed.

The call notes, or possibly single-note components within the songs, may be more important as isolating mechanisms than the full songs themselves. Certainly the calls, like the songs, are distinctive. The call of the Eastern Meadowlark is a buzzy note, vaguely suggesting the call of the Common Nighthawk or the American Woodcock. The call of the Western is lower-pitched, more abrupt, and clucklike.

In North America, the Western Meadowlark's range is steadily expanding to the east. On average, the Western Meadowlark prefers drier grasslands than those favored by the eastern species, but there are fields and meadows where both occur. Hybrids sometimes occur where the two species come together. Birds may experience confusion in learning the appropriate songs in habitats where one species' neighbors may be the other species.

In the population of Eastern Meadowlarks that occurs in northern South America, where there are no Western Meadowlarks, there is a curious variant in the song. It is still identifiably that of an Eastern Meadowlark, but on the end is often added a warbling cluster of notes, not unlike what is heard from the Western Meadowlark. Since there are no Western Meadowlarks living in the region, there is no need for a song that clearly distinguishes one species from the other. In areas of sympatry, where two similar species come together, there is a greater need for species-defining characters.

A Southern Eastern Meadowlark
In general, birds living in more arid regions tend to be paler than those living in greener, more humid regions. This applies to a race of the Eastern Meadowlark, *Sturnella magna lilianae,* found in the dry American Southwest and adjacent northwestern Mexico. Its song, while different in minor details, certainly favors the Eastern Meadowlark sound type. As well, as

*For birds and birders alike, song is more distinctive than appearance in distinguishing the Eastern Meadowlark (*Sturnella magna magna*), the upper figure, from the distinctive subspecies of the desert grasslands of southern Texas, Arizona, and Mexico (*S. m. lilianae*), middle figure, and from the Western Meadowlark (*S. neglecta*), bottom figure, which sings its own sweet song throughout much of western North America.*

in the other races of the Eastern Meadowlark, the yellow on the throat does not extend up toward the cheek.

However, *S. m. lilianae* is generally paler than the Eastern Meadowlark. It appears that environmental factors are involved in producing the paler appearance. The race *S. m. lilianae* is possibly converging with, or developing characteristics similar to those of, the Western Meadowlark in response to common environmental factors. To the degree that voice and appearance either have diverged, or will diverge still more in the future, from other races of the Eastern Meadowlark, appearance and/or—more likely—voice may serve increasingly as an isolating mechanism toward the production of a third species. Indeed, some scientists have already split *S. m. lilianae* from the Eastern Meadowlark as a separate species. The American Ornithologists Union seeks to standardize North American bird names, and I suspect that in the near future it may recognize *S. m. lilianae* as a distinct species.

Red-winged Blackbirds

The Red-winged Blackbird is a heavily studied Icterid species that breeds in every state except Hawaii, as far east as Nova Scotia, and as far south as Costa Rica. Red-wings may be found in a variety of habitats, particularly in fall and winter, but tule reed beds and stands of cattails are among their favorite nesting habitats. Although they may be found in extensive marshes, often just a tiny patch of cattails in a ditch is enough to attract some territorial Red-winged Blackbirds.

Traveling about the continent in the spring, a birder who takes the time to listen and make comparisons will find considerable regional variation in the song of the Red-winged Blackbird. To the degree that they are consistent, these variations may be called dialects. Red-winged Blackbirds are oscines, and there is also recognizable individual variation within a distinctive dialect zone.

The male Red-winged Blackbird's territorial song is linked to a visual display that, to varying degrees, features the bright scarlet lesser wing coverts, or epaulets. These feathers are fluffed as the wings are partly or almost completely spread and the bird tilts forward and utters, as if with some effort, the familiar *chonch-la-reeeeeee* song. There is much individual variation of song, but usually there is a preliminary burbling jumble of notes followed by a thin, drawn-out, more or less raspy note. The accompanying visual flourish is strictly a testosterone-driven "guy thing," with one male trying to show other males that his epaulets are better than theirs.

In an experiment where the red on one male was painted black, that male was pushed around by the other males. Thus the display, in its natural form, creates a balancing act whereby both the intensity of the display, over which the male has control, and the intensity of the color, over which he has no control, dictate the reaction of the opposing male.

In terms of communicating with females, voice alone is enough. A single male Red-winged Blackbird may try to attract two or more females to his harem, but the marsh-breeding habits of the species tend to facilitate the formation of loose colonies. Where there is one male Red-winged Blackbird with his harem, there are likely to be other such groupings.

The birds clearly recognize their neighbors by their vocalizations. Indeed, even breeding success is linked to such recognition. When recorded calls of males from other colonies are substituted for those of familiar neighbors, breeding success is lowered. Presumably this is because the assumed presence of strangers, as identified by their calls, increases stress at the expense of energy directed toward successful nesting. Thus males appear to be more comfortable in competition with the males they know than with newcomers, both of which are identified by their vocalizations.

Females respond to males with their own vocalizations. They also respond to the sounds of other females, although with a different type of call. During experiments using recordings, if the introductory notes of the male's song were removed, the female's response was reduced. On the other hand, neighboring males are less likely to respond to the introductory notes than to the longer endnote of a neighboring male's song. The part of the male's territorial song of more interest to the female thus appears to be different from the part that is more important to neighboring males. It seems that females instinctively analyze and respond to a greater part of the male's territorial call than do neighboring males.

Males normally arrive on their territories ahead of the females. In the absence of females, males are inclined to exercise a smaller portion of their limited song repertoires than after females arrive. Evidence indicates that females are more sensitive to more variety in the male song than are other males and prefer a greater, rather than lesser, number of song types and variations. On the other hand, the absence of females is likely to promote an increase in the number of times the male sings. It is as if the male sings more to make sure that he is found by the females as they arrive, but once females have arrived, he sings fewer songs with greater variety, as variety is what they appear to appreciate.

That females are more sensitive to the male's song than are other males was demonstrated by an experiment in which male and female Red-winged Blackbirds' reactions to the song of a male Red-winged Blackbird and to a Northern Mockingbird's mimicked version of the same song were compared. The females were four times less likely to be fooled than the males.

Why the difference? Put simply, the song is more important as an isolating mechanism for the female than for the male. If the female mates with the wrong species, the cost to her is her brood for that season. If the male were to make a similar mistake, it would not matter in terms of his genetic contribution to brood production, other than some lost time. The female therefore has more at stake in being able to accurately identify the source of a song.

Male Red-winged Blackbirds with larger repertoires will have more mates, on average, than those with fewer songs. Variety in song types apparently facilitates infidelity on behalf of the male. A male Red-wing with lots of song types is more attractive to females and is thus more likely to breed with the mate of a neighboring male than is a competitor with a smaller range of vocalization. While each male attempts to maintain a harem of "his" females, both sexes are likely to stray, and it is estimated that as many as one in five of the male's matings are with females outside his harem.

The other crucial factor in Red-winged Blackbird mating success is quality of the territory chosen. The brightest colored—and therefore the most successful at challenging other males—male Red-winged Blackbirds with the largest numbers of mates have territories toward the center of the marsh, where optimal habitat generally occurs. Both vocal repertoire and quality of territory determine a male's attractiveness to females, while quality of visual display determines his ability to defend both territory and females from rival males.

Availability of food is another factor in Red-winged Blackbird male song production. While it is unclear how much energy is used in singing, it obviously requires time that is subtracted from other activities. Low food

The Red-winged Blackbird is one of the most studied of all songbirds. The male's breeding song is closely linked to a display featuring his red epaulets. The streaked female has her own song. The species is found throughout most of North America.

Barry Kent MacKay

availability can have a negative impact on how much time is spent on singing versus foraging. In experiments in which abundant food was provided, Red-winged Blackbirds sang with greater frequency.

As with many other bird species, seasonal enlargements in the parts of the brain controlling song have been found in the male Red-winged Blackbird, with some parts of the brain being up to 70 percent larger in breeding—and singing—birds than in nonbreeding birds. The size of the individual repertoire is modest, up to six songs in a single male, but it seems to increase from season to season. However, the size of the part of the brain that controls song output does not increase with the increase in song repertoire.

There is some indication that the timing of songs is determined by the colony's dominant male or males, with the others following, sequentially, the lead set by one or more birds. Interestingly, a frequent neighbor of the Red-winged Blackbird, the Marsh Wren, has been observed displaying the same follow-the-leader type of singing.

A male Red-winged Blackbird that cannot sing is far more likely to have his territory invaded by neighboring males and must resort to an increase in visual displays in an effort to protect his territory.

The Yellow-rumped Cacique

It is interesting to compare the situation with the Red-winged Blackbird to that of another member of the same family, Icteridae: the Yellow-rumped Cacique. The Yellow-rumped Cacique has a huge range throughout much of tropical South America. It is common, colorfully conspicuous, noisy, and therefore very hard to miss.

The male cacique also maintains a harem. However, male caciques spend so much time and energy trying to prevent their mates from going astray or rival males from seducing the ladies that the poor birds may weaken, only to be replaced by more vigorous males.

The Andes isolate two populations of the Yellow-rumped Cacique. To the east of the Andes, the species, noteworthy for its wide range of calls, is an accomplished mimic. This is the nominate race, *Cacicus cela cela*. The males in a colony all sing the same song variant within that colony. That song variant may change prior to the end of the nesting season, but all males will make the same change and so will still be singing the same song. One song may last as long as twenty minutes and contain a bewildering variety of notes and imitations of other birds, frogs, and insects. There is also a "harsh" song that contains the *tchak* notes that are so

The male Yellow-rumped Cacique may expend so much energy on
vocalizations and displays to maintain his "harem" that he becomes
exhausted and is replaced by a stronger male. This conspicuous species
is widely distributed in South America.

distinctive of this species. The female rarely sings the long song and apparently never sings the harsh song.

To the west of the Andes, a different subspecies of the Yellow-rumped Cacique, *C. c. flavicrissus,* apparently is not a mimic at all. Presumably, mimicry confers an advantage to birds on the east side of the Andes, where there are greater numbers of bird species, than it does on the west side. It is possible that mimicry evolved after the two populations were separated, or perhaps it was an ability that, having less value to the western birds, for whatever reason, died out.

Isolating Mechanisms

The major purpose of birdsong is to assist in obtaining a mate. Thus song serves as an essential isolating mechanism.

There can be other isolating mechanisms as well, including physical barriers, markings, displays, habitat preferences, and so on—anything that serves to help keep species from interbreeding, as hybridization tends to produce less viable offspring. ∎

A third race, *C. c. vitellinus,* is found in Panama and parts of Colombia. It is not a mimic either, and its repertoire lacks the harsh, metallic sounds of *C. c. flavicrissus.* Colonies that are close to each other tend to share similar song types. The farther separated the colonies, the less the song types resemble each other. All males share about five to eight song types, and all males within the colony sing the same song type at the same time. The structure of these shared songs changes through time. Studies in Panama indicate that certain song types may be associated with certain behaviors or social contexts.

SIX

Bird Sounds

The types of sound birds use to communicate are driven by the process of selection, including sexual selection. The quality and nature of some sounds, such as contact calls, may contribute to the survival of the individual or its offspring, whereas the quality and nature of other sounds, such as territorial songs, may contribute to successful breeding. The inheritable traits that contribute to survival and to successful breeding are passed on to the next generation. To us, the results can be the joyously complex serenade of a mockingbird. To the bird, sound is a means of perpetuation. Those traits that help distinguish one species from another are selected for. Thus a House Wren's song attracts female House Wrens but not female Sedge Wrens, and will challenge male House Wrens but not elicit responses from male Sedge Wrens.

Repertoire

The term *repertoire* in reference to avian vocalization usually refers to the number of distinct song types uttered by a given individual of a songbird species. Thus, one individual within a species may have a larger or smaller repertoire than another. The term may also refer to the number of song types that may be found within a species, particularly a songbird. Among songbirds, the Brown Thrasher of North America is probably the song repertoire record holder, a single individual having been recorded with more than two thousand songs, though that does not necessarily mean that every Brown Thrasher has an equally large repertoire.

In nonsongbirds, the degree of variety of sound production is typically more limited, although some species may display a bewildering diversity of individual calls and note combinations. A biologist studying the Willow

Ptarmigan, a grouse species, once told me that it almost seemed as though the sounds and combinations of noises the birds produced might be limitless, so varied they were.

Duet, Antiphonal, and Synchronous Singing

Duetting and synchronous or antiphonal singing are terms used in an attempt to establish boundaries within the dynamic fluidity of evolving behavior. Duet vocalization is typically antiphonal, with each of two birds singing separate parts that, in combination, make up a complete song. The result typically gives the impression of being a single song from one bird, unless the listener is positioned between the two singers and thus can hear the separate contributions. Birds also may duet by application of mechanical, or instrumental, sounds, as when a pair of storks respond to each other with bill rattling. Singing is synchronous when both birds sing or call the same phrase or note at the same time.

Many bird species call or sing in chorus, with many of them vocalizing either antiphonally or synchronously. Birds may indulge in unison calling, where two or more individuals utter the same call—or similar calls, given gender-based differences in pitch—sequentially or with overlap, possibly with the second call being started before the first is complete.

While duetting is usually territorial singing that contributes to strong pair bonding, there are various reasons why two or more birds sing together. There may be uncoordinated vocal or mechanical noise making among groups of rivals, or contact notes and calls keeping groups of birds together while possibly reinforcing flock bonding. The alarm call of one species may trigger different alarm calls of other species.

An Interspecific Duet

The Fork-tailed, or Common, Drongo is a familiar bird throughout much of Africa. It is noteworthy for a variety of often less-than-musical notes in its song. A pair of drongos will sometimes sing a synchronous duet. One drongo was observed in duet with a Slate-colored Boubou. As its name implies, this species of bush-shrike is a dull black color. The drongo is also black, although with slightly glossy plumage. Both birds share dry shrub habitat. In this instance, the drongo adjusted its calling to accommodate the bush-shrike. Genders of the two birds were unknown. Such flexibility is presumably a key to songbird duet singing, in which new songs are forever being developed.

Bush-shrike Duets

The bush-shrikes, a family of oscines native to Africa, contain some of the most studied duet singers. The female of one species, the Black-headed Gonolek, has been found to have a response time of only 144 milliseconds in reply to her mate's song. Such reflexes exceed human capability.

Luhder's Bush-Shrike is a handsome bird that tends to keep out of sight in shrubs and thickets. The song is a liquid whistling, with the male and female uttering alternating, rolling strings of notes, the sound of one following the other so rapidly that the resulting song seems to be a seamlessly single performance.

In the 1960s, studies involving a close relative of the Luhder's Bush-Shrike, the more widely distributed Tropical Boubou, found that a duet might start with either of the pair. Songs by trios of birds have been recorded as well. The tones are in exact pitch and of such purity that three-part songs have been rendered in musical notes, with different birds' contributions to the composition indicated.

Nonpasserine Duet and Group Singing

Bush-shrikes may have among the most precise of duets, but duetting and chorus singing also occur among a wide variety of unrelated bird species. Barbets, which are nonpasserines, are noted for duetting and chorus singing. As might be expected of nonpasserines, the songs are far more uniform within the species than is the case with bush-shrikes and other duet-singing passerines.

Red-fronted Barbets, native to Africa, have a rather loud, simple call—*hoop-hoop-hoop-hoop*—with up to fifteen such notes uttered in succession, either by one bird or as a duet. The song of the Black-collared Barbet, also of Africa, is a lively antiphonal duet, with a *kee* note by one bird followed by a *pup-up* note by the other member of the pair.

Other birds for which some form of duet singing has been recorded include, but are far from limited to, the kiwis, Little Grebe, Pied-billed Grebe, Marbled Wood-Quail, forest-falcons, Bar-tailed Trogon, Laughing Kookaburra, various babblers, various tyrant-flycatchers, California Thrasher, various wrens, Buff-rumped Warbler, and Buff-throated Saltator.

There are many others, and undoubtedly still more will be discovered, particularly as close attention is paid to the songs of tropical birds. Many birds sing duets within thick vegetation, where it can be difficult to see whether two singers are involved. The singers are often relatively sedentary, and unless the listener is properly situated, their closely synchronized or antiphonal songs will seem to originate with but one bird. Duet singers are usually found in tropical and subtropical regions where there may be little ornithological investigation. Because duet singing is relatively rare among birds in temperate climates, early field workers from such regions may not have been looking for such cases when they explored distant regions.

Choral singing is far easier to detect. Bell Miners, native to eastern Australia, are olive-colored oscines that gather in flocks noteworthy for their continued tinkling calls. On the leaf-littered floor of Australia's northern rain forests, groups of Chowchillas continually cackle, dominating the dawn chorus with calls rendered *chow-chilla* or *chowry-chook-chook*.

Singing Other Songs

In November 1998, an American birder commented on the Internet that she had heard a Baltimore Oriole sing the song of a Tufted Titmouse. The two species' songs are not alike, and orioles are not considered to be mimics. In June 1999, my friend Ron Tozer reported that for the third consecutive year he encountered a male Yellow-rumped Warbler that sang a Prairie Warbler–like song in Algonquin Park, Ontario. The song was so similar to that of the Prairie Warbler that several birders so reported it, basing their identification only on the voice, even though the Prairie Warbler has never been found in Algonquin Park. "I played a tape of the Prairie Warbler to this unusual Yellow-rumped," reported Tozer, "and it actually approached me and scolded and sang vigorously. . . . In my experience, observations of warblers singing a song like another species are rare, and normally are not 'perfect' imitations. However, it is always worthwhile to 'visually check' any songs that sound odd, or involve species out of range or normal habitat—just in case!"

Whereas songbirds combine instinct and learning to produce their most complex vocalizations, sometimes even learning the song of a different species, the nonpasserines tend to produce sound instinctively, with little or no learning. However, there is often much individual variation among nonpasserine species. Northern Gannets, for example, nest in large colonies, placing nests on cliff ledges or headlands. Each nest is situated about the distance the birds can reach with their sharply edged and pointed beaks. Although they fly and dive with grace and precision, these goose-size seabirds land rather awkwardly, and none too accurately, amid the throngs of noisy and aggressive neighbors. Amid the confusion, the adult birds are able to find the distinctive calls of their own young among large numbers of similar chicks.

In one family of seabirds, the Alcids, there is typically a period of separation between parents and chicks, followed by a reunion. In these birds, a parent needs to be able to distinguish its own chick, or else adopt some other chick as its own. By marking chicks and parents, field biologists have discovered that the parent birds are able to recognize their own chicks.

The Ancient Murrelet, a stocky little Alcid, nests in tunnels dug in the turf off coastal woodlands of the North Pacific, from Korea to British Columbia. Each tunnel may be as long as 2 or 3 feet, with a nest chamber at the end about 5 inches across and 2 or 3 inches deep. Each female lays two (sometimes only one) egg. All the babies in the various burrows hatch about the same time. They spend three to five days in the nest chamber without eating. Then, under cover of darkness, they lurch and waddle out of the tunnel and head seaward, traveling perhaps 300 meters or more over terrain that to a small, downy chick can be quite hazardous. Some colonies may contain thousands, even tens of thousands, of nests. Thus there may be a mass, nocturnal emigration of flightless, hungry chicks swarming over branches and rocks, instinctively seeking the relative safety of the ocean. They enter the sea immediately, swimming buoyantly.

Waiting on the water, in the darkness, are thousands of parent birds. There, in the waves, wind, and gloom, amid the frantic mob of chicks, the parent birds are able to detect the distinctive calls of their own youngsters.

Doves and Pigeons: Vocal Variations

Songbirds require learning to perfect their songs. But what of nonpasserine species? What would happen if the young bird of one species was placed in the nest of an entirely different species? Doves and pigeons are nonpasserines with distinctive vocalizations. Researchers have placed the young of one dove species in the nest of another dove species. This simple experiment demonstrated that the foster baby dove grows up using its biological parents' vocalizations. So far as scientists have determined to date, songbirds require their own species as role models.

Playback experiments using high-fidelity recordings have shown that young Mourning Doves, a species abundant in North America, may recognize their own father by the distinctiveness of the calls he utters upon visits to the nest. That does not suggest that the young birds emulate or learn from the parent or that the calls are not inherent. However, it does show that the calls of all individuals are not necessarily identical, or so similar as to be indiscernible to other members of the species. Variation may be subtle and minimal compared with what is experienced with oscines, but it is not lacking.

Experiments with captive doves have shown that when two closely related species are hybridized, the call of the resulting hybrid resembles that of one of the parent species. Thus the offspring of a mating between a Tambourine Dove, an African species of the genus *Turtur,* and a Namaqua Dove, another African species of the same genus, gave the call of the father, the Tambourine Dove.

Because the calls of nonpasserines are inherent, however, they can be wrecked by hybridization. The hybrid chick receives genes from two different species. When two quite unrelated species are hybridized, the process results in the mature hybrid having vocalizations that completely match those of neither parent species. When a Socorro Dove, a highly endangered member of the New World genus *Zenaida,* was mated to an unrelated African Collared-Dove of the genus *Streptopelia,* the call of the resulting offspring did not resemble that of either parent species.

Echolocation

The interiors of caves where Edible-nest Swiftlets nest are often quite dark. The birds fly quickly, and they often hunt at twilight. Feeding can be a frenzied affair, when the Edible-nest Swiftlets swarm in massed flocks with other swifts and swallows.

The Edible-nest Swiftlet emits a string of high-pitched notes that bounce off objects and rebound to the bird's ears. The length of time it takes for the sound to return lets the bird determine the distance of the object, and the quality of the sound reveals features about the size and shape of the object. This is echolocation—the same process used by bats, similar in principle to radar and sonar.

Several other species of swiftlets are either thought to or known to echolocate, including the Seychelles, Mascarene, Indian, Mountain, White-rumped, Australian, Himalayan, Mossy-nest, Uniform, Sawtell's, Polynesian, and Black-nest Swiftlets, and doubtless others that have been too little studied to determine whether they use echolocation. In some species, it appears that some races practice echolocation while others do not.

Oilbirds

In 1799 the naturalist-explorer Alexander von Humboldt visited Caripe, in northern Venezuela, where the locals told him of a most extraordinary bird that lived in a cave. Humboldt brought the existence of this unique bird—the Oilbird—to the attention of science.

The Oilbird is an elongated, dark mahogany-rufous, long-winged bird with a stout beak, small feet, and large eyes. It is placed in its own family, Steatornithidae, related to nightjars and Whip-poor-wills. Oilbirds feed on the strongly scented fruits of palms, laurels of the family Lauraceae, and incense (Burseraceae)—all obtained within 10 or 15 miles of their nesting colony. They hover beneath the masses of fruit, picking them off, sometimes in the company of large fruit bats. Like the bats, they are nocturnal.

An Oilbird's voice is grating and noisy. Usually the birds are silent, but if disturbed in the cave they can mount a deafening racket that reverberates through the cavern. It was first demonstrated in 1954 that the birds do use echolocation to fly in dark caves. Like the echolocation calls of some larger bat species, the Oilbird's echolocation calls are not quite ultrasonic, thus audible to humans. It is also apparent that the Oilbirds use smell to help locate at least some of the fruit they consume. The eyes are large, and once outside the cave the Oilbird usually uses echolocation only when flying in the extreme darkness beneath the forest canopy.

SEVEN

Brood Parasites

Brood parasites are birds—some passerines, some not—that lay their eggs in the nests of other bird species. The unwitting host species raises the unrelated youngster. Obviously the young passerine parasite cannot learn the song of its own species from its parents. In nonpasserine species, the begging call may not be recognized as such by host parents of a quite different species.

The Black-headed Duck, native to South America, is a brood parasite that lays its eggs in the nests of other duck species, depending on them to raise its young. The contact calls, appearance, and behavior of baby ducklings of various species are similar enough that many duck species will raise the young of other species. In fact, from time to time, other species of ducks will, apparently by accident, lay their eggs in the wrong nest, or orphan ducklings will fit into a

Canadian owl expert Kay McKeever once conducted an experiment with a very maternal captive Spectacled Owl, a species native to Central and South America. The bird, whose name was Granny, was particularly useful as a surrogate or foster parent to orphaned young owls of quite different species brought to McKeever's owl sanctuary to be raised and rehabilitated to the wild. Granny was presented with a chicken's egg.

The chick hatched, equipped with all the contact and food begging calls of his decidedly un-owl-like species. The owl, a natural potential predator of such birds as chickens, accepted the chick as one of her own, feeding him meat. The chick

continued on page 76

brood of a different species without any apparent major difficulty.

Other brood parasites have evolved elaborate means of fooling host species into raising their young, reducing or eliminating competition from the host's biological offspring, and of dealing with the absence of role models of their own species.

Honeyguides

Honeyguides are members of the nonpasserine family Indicatoridae, native to sub-Saharan Africa and southern Asia. Each species tends to specialize in a small range of host species. Scaley-throated Honeyguides only parasitize woodpeckers, for example.

thrived on the diet, and neither bird gave any indication of experiencing anything other than a typical parent-chick relationship.

The fact that the chick entered Granny's life from an egg she was incubating overwhelmed all the inherent visual, audio, and behavioral differences between a baby rooster and a baby Spectacled Owl. This was a demonstration of something called brood parasitism, commonly practiced by a wide variety of bird species.

Greater Honeyguides choose starlings, rollers, or bee-eaters as host species, and the Lesser Honeyguide lays eggs in the nests of either woodpeckers or large barbets. Such hosts are also nonpasserines, but the Whalberg's Honeybird and the closely related Cassin's Honeybird, both members of the genus *Prodotiscus,* utilize passerine hosts. Honeyguides of the genus *Indicator* lay eggs either in host nests that are located in cavities or in host nests that are globular. The advantage is that the host parent cannot clearly see the parasite chick. The honeybirds, which are small honeyguides of the genus *Prodotiscus,* may choose to lay eggs in nests that are open.

Honeyguides have developed brutally efficient means of succeeding as brood parasites. The chicks are hatched with a sharp hook at the tip of the beak. Even though they are naked, blind, and relatively helpless, they use the hook to kill the young of the host species. Being nonoscines, they have no need to learn adult songs.

Calls of Brood Parasites

All indigobirds, a group of remarkably similar tiny, glossy, dark blue-black whydahs also found in Africa, are brood parasites. The Purple Indigobird usually lays her eggs in the nest of the Jameson's Firefinch. Adults of the two species are entirely dissimilar, but newly hatched young of the two species have the same mouth patterns, which the parent bird sees when feeding babies.

If parent birds provide the song role model for young birds, what happens with indigobirds raised by foster parent hosts? In fact, the indigobird nestlings learn the song of the host species. A Purple Indigobird raised by Jameson's Firefinches learns the song of the Jameson's Firefinch, while maintaining songs that are specific to indigobirds. The *purr* note of the firefinch consists of about twenty-two notes per second and is closely imitated by the Purple Indigobird. The Jameson's Firefinch develops regional dialects through its wide range. The pattern of such regional song dialects found in the host species, the firefinch, is also found in the adult Purple Indigobird.

Sometimes a Purple Indigobird is raised by a different host species—not the usual Jameson's Firefinch—and when that happens, the young bird, upon maturity, sings quite a different song from most others of its kind, influenced by its host. The whole thing depends on the adult indigobirds responding appropriately to the songs, even though the same song (but not the physical appearance) is shared by two separate species.

By mating with a male bird that sings like the species in whose nest she will lay her eggs, there is a correspondingly increased assurance that the mouth markings of her offspring will match those of the hatchlings of the host species.

However, indigobird songs are intensely varied. There are songs that don't imitate the host species but are specific to different areas.

The widely distributed Village Indigobird parasitizes the Red-billed Firefinch, and thus adult males incorporate the Red-billed Firefinch's song in their own large repertoire, with each male having twenty or more song types. The Variable Indigobird parasitizes, and imitates, the African Firefinch. The male Steel-blue Whydah looks like an indigobird, except that in breeding plumage, it sports four slender, greatly elongated central tail feathers. Also, unlike indigobirds, it has white under the wings and a patch of white on the back, usually concealed when the bird is perched. It is unclear whether it imitates its host species, but it will pick up various finch songs, as well as use an inherent repertoire.

Cowbirds

All cowbird species except one are brood parasites. The exception is the Bay-winged Cowbird of southern and central South America. It raises its own young, although it often does so in a nest usurped from another songbird species. Such nest expropriation is believed to be a very early stage in the ultimate development of brood parasitism. In regions where both the Bay-winged and the Screaming Cowbird occur, the Bay-winged Cowbird is normally the single, or obligate, host species of the Screaming Cowbird. The baby Screaming Cowbird's begging calls are very similar to the begging calls of the chicks of the usual host species, the Bay-winged Cowbird.

The Giant Cowbird, widely distributed throughout much of Central and South America, lays its eggs in the nests of colonial caciques or oropendolas. The Giant Cowbird is apparently silent—a songbird without a song.

Generally speaking, in songbird species, the young male first learns from exposure to the songs of adult males—father or neighbors. In the Brown-headed Cowbird, widely distributed through much of North America, the learning happens in conjunction with song development, in response to the female's reactions.

Briefly, the brood parasites that lay their eggs in the nests of a single species, or in the nests of several related species, have a greater likelihood of a match but must find the appropriate host. Species like the Brown-headed Cowbird, which will lay eggs in almost any open nest, face much more rejection of their eggs or young but have a great many more options to choose from.

The begging calls of the baby Brown-headed Cowbird can't possibly match those of all potential host species, and so it is important for there to be minimal competition for the host parent's attention. A host faced with a choice between her own young and an alien might make the wrong choice, from the intruder's perspective. Thus female cowbirds often throw out at least some of the eggs of the host. The baby cowbird is often bigger and stronger than the host's own babies and crowds them out of the nest.

The song of the Brown-headed Cowbird is accompanied by a dramatic visual display. As he sings his brief song, the male bird awkwardly tilts forward, half spreading his wings and fluffing his shiny, iridescent, steel-blue body plumage as he utters a series of strangled, gurgling notes. The song is abrupt and has the distinction of covering four octaves, thus being spread over a greater range of frequency than the song of any other bird. The Bobolink's cheerful song comes close, however, and is much more musical to human ears.

The young cowbird lacks the opportunity to learn the song of the parent birds or of neighboring cowbird males singing on territory. This is also true of the indigobirds. What is different is the fact that the Brown-headed Cowbird may attempt to parasitize any of more than one hundred different host species. Some species, such as the American Robin, will usually toss out the cowbird eggs. If a Yellow Warbler finds a cowbird's egg in her nest, she will build a false floor above it and lay a new clutch.

It appears that the Brown-headed Cowbird's song must be inherited, but it's not quite that simple. While the male cowbird may be able to draw upon his hard-wired, instinctive template in order to produce the basic structure of the song, he is, like other songbirds, able to refine his song. To do this, he requires the reaction of the songless female.

The female cowbird has a wing-stroking display that consists of the wings being held out from the body and moved up and down. This display serves to stimulate the male. Thus, the better the male song, the better the female's reinforcing reaction. The female does not respond to every male. The male's song must be right in order to elicit the display. The males have a dominance order reflected by their song-and-display ability.

The female's wing-stroking is a form of submissive display that is common among courting birds. Prior to mating, females will crouch and flutter wings very much as do young birds begging for food. In turn, the male is stimulated to display and, ultimately, copulate. Many bird species, both passerine and nonpasserine, carry the display further to engage in courtship feeding.

Cuckoos

Cuckoos are nonpasserines. The Common, or Eurasian, Cuckoo has caused the family to achieve widespread recognition both for its call and for its brood parasitism. Approximately fifty cuckoo species are brood parasites. The remaining eighty-six species of cuckoos usually lay their eggs in their own nests and raise their own young. The female cuckoo seeks to deceive the birds of other species in whose nests she lays her eggs.

In the interest of removing competition, the newly hatched cuckoo instinctively pushes against its host's eggs or babies, bracing with feet and wings, pushing them up the side of the nest and over the top. This removes competition for the host's attention.

Sometimes the female cuckoo, prior to laying her egg, removes one or more of the host's eggs, or she may remove or eat all of the eggs from the nest of a songbird, whether or not she subsequently uses the nest for her own egg. The young of some brood-parasite cuckoos, such as the Common Koel, may coexist with those of the host species.

The most studied of the brood-parasitizing cuckoos is the Common Cuckoo. The species is found across Europe and Asia, including parts of

North Africa. The male's call, *CUCK-koo* or *KWA-cuck-koo*, inspiration for passages in Beethoven's "Pastoral Symphony" and for Swiss cuckoo clocks alike, is one of the world's most distinctive and widely identifiable bird sounds. The female utters a higher-pitched, bubbling series of notes.

Unlike the indigobirds, the mature cuckoo's vocalization is independent of learning from its hosts, because the cuckoo is a nonpasserine. Like the Brown-headed Cowbird, the Common Cuckoo is widely distributed, occurs in various habitats, and benefits from having a wide selection of host species.

The Common Cuckoo is a little more devious than the cowbird. Common Cuckoos lay eggs of specific colors and patterns in the nests of species that have eggs of similar colors and patterns. This is called egg mimicry. Thus a cuckoo that produces eggs colored like those of a Common Redstart tends to lay in a Common Redstart's nest. A cuckoo that produces eggs colored like those of a wagtail usually lays in a wagtail's nest.

Recent studies show that the baby cuckoo's begging calls play a major role in the deception. Some hosts will wear themselves ragged trying to feed the constantly begging baby. A baby cuckoo has the ability to imitate the plaintive food-begging sound of the songbird babies—not just one baby songbird begging for food, but a nest full. The actual songbird babies themselves are long gone, ejected by the cuckoo hatchling perhaps before they even hatched.

New studies indicate that the young cuckoo inherently imitates the sound of songbird babies' collective food-begging notes. Thus, in addition to visual egg mimicry, the Common Cuckoo is capable of audio brood mimicry. Songbird chicks, when satiated, stop opening their mouths and stop peeping. Cuckoo babies don't stop begging for food.

The unwitting hosts of baby cuckoos are frequently small birds, several times smaller than the young cuckoo. The foster parents often work extraordinarily hard to meet the incessant demands for food made upon them by the young Common Cuckoo.

The single parasite may consume more than an entire brood of the host's own babies would have devoured in the same amount of time. It has been assumed that the larger size of the cuckoo provides the stimulus that promotes the exhausting effort of the host species.

However, some experiments involving the placement of nestlings of larger but nonparasitical species, such as European Blackbirds, into nests of smaller birds indicated that increased size did not trigger the "high-gear" feeding response elicited by young cuckoos. The young European Blackbirds did not receive preferential treatment.

EIGHT

Communication Among Species

A hunting Sharp-shinned Hawk, recognizing that its image conveys its presence, seeks to keep out of sight as it hunts, often in woods and forests. This bird-hunting species very much depends on the element of surprise to obtain its ever-alert prey. Thus it is silent when hunting. Small birds, upon perceiving such danger, usually give alarm notes. It is in the hawk's interest not to be seen or heard. If alarm notes are uttered, other birds will approach and also give alarm notes, betraying the presence of the raptor.

Another raptor, the Slaty-backed Forest-Falcon, native to forests of South America, also tries to keep hidden from its prey. Most falcons have long, pointed wings and fly swiftly in open areas, but forest-falcons have rounded wings suitable for quick maneuverability in thick vegetation. In this, the forest-falcons resemble the Sharp-shinned Hawk and its close relatives. However, unlike the Sharp-shinned Hawk, the forest-falcon employs vocalization to lure prey within striking range. The predator makes sounds like the mobbing calls of birds that have found a predator. Small birds of a variety of species will, upon hearing avian alarm notes, fly close to join in mobbing behavior, wherein the birds flit about the perched owl, hawk, snake, or cat and badger it while alerting all other small birds to its presence. The Slaty-backed Forest-Falcon, while sitting obscured by forest cover, makes calls that will draw birds close. Suddenly the falcon emerges from hiding to snatch a meal. The deceit apparently works better on visiting migrants from North America, unused to the ways of the jungle raptor, than on native small birds.

Mixed Flocks

Mixed flocks are flocks of birds of different species. Such flocks may scatter through a woodland or other habitat, with many members out of sight of each other. Mixed flocks of shorebirds or waterfowl may consist of various birds of two or more species in a rather sharply defined assembly, close together. Contact may be audio, visual, or most likely, both.

Mixed flocks may also consist of migrating birds of various species traveling more or less together. Some such associations, as when one sees several species of raptors migrating at the same time, may reflect the fact that the birds are all benefiting from local weather conditions that facilitate soaring.

But the term also applies to groups of birds found in less sharply defined groupings, for whom companionship of individuals of various species confers mutual benefits. In the endless process of finding food and detecting predators, the more eyes and ears, the better. In much of North America and Eurasia, members of the chickadee and tit family will, in winter woodlands, be the first members of a mixed flock to be noticed by a birder. Species such as the Black-capped Chickadee, found throughout most of North America, are very energetic and noisy little birds as they move through the tree branches with acrobatic agility. Nuthatches, kinglets, creepers, and perhaps the odd Downy Woodpecker may associate with them. A characteristic of such mixed flocks is that usually only a part of the assembly is in view at any one time as the birds move slowly through various parts of the woods, maintaining audio or visual contact with others in the group.

The chickadee may be a nuclear species that attracts others with its calls. On visits to the higher cloud forests of Central America, I learned to look and listen for Sooty-capped Bush-tanagers. They are nuclear species that, as they move through mossy woodlands in flocks of five to twenty, attract Collared Redstarts, Ruddy Treerunners, and other small birds. In the Amazon rain forests, three closely related suboscines, the Bluish-slate, Cinereous, and Dusky-throated Antshrikes have special calls they use to attract birds of other species. The song of the Cinereous Antshrike has been described as commencing with "several wheezy whistled notes," which rapidly accelerate to end in a long, bubbling trill, *whee, whee, whee-whee-whee-wheep-wheepwhipwhipwhip-p-p-p-p-p-pr.* The song is loud and distinctive and indicates to birds and birders alike that there may be a mixed flock of forest birds nearby. Sometimes the antshrikes will flit ahead of other birds and call, as if urging them on.

I recall my initial frustration when, as one of three trip leaders, I took some birders into a forest in Costa Rica. For many, it was their first experience in a tropical forest. There were no birds at all. It was easy to overload the visual senses on a bewildering array of leaf shapes, sizes, and colors, looking for some bird—any bird! I could hear dark mumbling about how much their ecotour had cost. They certainly weren't getting their money's worth. After about twenty minutes of fruitless searching, everyone was so solemn that I decided to play a bit of a joke, quietly calling, "Here birds; here birds." It was shortly after that, by pure luck (perhaps aided by the laws of probability), that a swarm of birds arrived. All disappointment was forgotten as tanagers, warblers, woodcreepers, honeycreepers, and some gnatcatchers were spotted in quick succession. "You didn't *really* call them, did you?" asked one incredulous client.

The attractions for such flocks vary. Fruiting trees, swarms of ants, or areas of seeds may attract wandering flocks of birds. Army ants are a particular source of interest to such flocks. The birds rarely eat the ants themselves, focusing instead on small reptiles, amphibians, and large various insects that are flushed from cover as they flee the voracious ants.

Such mixed flocks maintain contact through low calls. This is a relatively simple but effective form of communication among species, known as interspecific communication.

Audio Communication of Information from Species to Species

There is a drab-colored bird species in Africa with the rather descriptive scientific name *Indicator indicator.* It looks like a songbird but is actually a nonpasserine. What does the bird indicate? The clue is in the bird's English name, Greater Honeyguide, or Black-throated Honeyguide.

The male Greater Honeyguide's usual territorial song is a monotonously repeated *Weeipp-churr* or *Wheeit-purr,* which has a rolling quality as it is repeated over and over again. The birds are always on the lookout for beehives, where there are wax and honey. The chopping of wood will attract them, as trees are sometimes felled to reach beehives. If a hive is found, the honeyguide appears very excited. Both sexes of Greater Honeyguides have a dry rattling or churring call that is highly distinctive, sounding like a bunch of wooden matches being rapidly shaken in a cardboard box. This is accompanied by much conspicuous tail flashing and fluttering about.

There is a honey-loving mammal that shares much of the Greater Honeyguide's African range. The Ratel is a thickset and strongly clawed mammal that is very light grizzled gray above and black below, the two colors being sharply demarcated. It looks superficially like a badger, and like badgers, it is a distinctive member of the weasel family. In addition to powerful front claws, the Ratel has very thick skin. Both adaptations allow it to indulge in its taste for wild honey with little concern about bee stings. The Ratel also eats large insects and some reptiles, including mambas—among the deadliest of poisonous snakes.

A charming legend holds that this mammal would follow honeyguides, to both parties' benefit. The Ratel would tear open the hive to eat the honey, while the bird would eat the wax. But there appears to be no basis for this tale. If there is any interspecific communication between these two species, it goes the other way—it is the Ratel's grunt that attracts the bird.

For most animals, wax is indigestible, but honeyguides, which have even been known to eat the wax of candles, can metabolize it, possibly because their intestines contain flora able to break down saturated, long-chain fatty acids. Or possibly the Honeyguide's wax-digesting ability is due to special physiological features such as those found in North American Yellow-rumped Warblers and Tree Swallows, which may eat large numbers of wax-coated bayberries during their fall migration along the U.S. East Coast.

Though the story of the Ratel following the honeyguide lacks substantiation, there is one mammal species that responds to the *churring* rattle of the Greater Honeyguide: humans. The honeyguide may seek out humans and, flashing their white tail feathers and bouncing about with great energy, they will give their call that signifies that they have found honey. It's not clear if they first find the honey and then the human, or first the human and then the honey. Possibly they do both. Honeyguides have been known to guide people directly, by the shortest route, to a beehive. However, they've also been known to "guide" a human over a rambling, circuitous route, as if trying to find a hive for the human to hack open.

Some folks are careful to take the honey the bird has led them to but leave the wax as reward for the honeyguide. Others think it better to remove the wax in order to keep the birds hungry and thus on the trail of still more beehives.

In the savannahs of northeast Africa, the Von der Decken's Hornbill interacts vocally with the Dwarf Mongoose, to the benefit of both.

Both sexes give the guiding call; however, the female will sometimes utter a *whit* or *wheet* call in response to barbets, which are often the unwitting hosts of this brood parasite.

Another Bird and Mammal Partnership

Von der Decken's Hornbill, found only in East Africa, is a member of the nonpasserine hornbill family Bucerotidae. The hornbill is a terrestrial feeder with a fondness for insects, snails, mice, baby birds, and other small animals. Typically, the hornbill perches above the ground, looking for prey, and then drops down to consume whatever it finds. Feeding depends on prey being visible.

The Dwarf Mongoose, native to the same region, lives in burrows. The mongoose actively hunts insects, small lizards, and other small animals, flushing them from cover. The hornbill takes its share of the organisms the mongoose exposes. In return, the hornbill acts as a lookout for both of them, sounding an alarm against predators, even ones that are solely a threat to the mongooses but not to the hornbills. This could be called inter-specific altruism, in that the bird warns the mammal without being at risk itself and without any immediate benefit, except that it's in the bird's long-term self-interest to reduce predation on Dwarf Mongooses.

The mongoose recognizes and responds to the presence of the hornbills, recognizes and responds to their alarm calls, and has its own ability to communicate with the hornbills. This hornbill-mongoose symbiotic relationship, also called mutualism, is also shared by the Eastern Yellow-billed Hornbill and the Dwarf Mongoose.

NINE

Birds Named for Their Sounds

It is difficult to describe birds' vocalizations in print. For example, to me, the Tennessee Warbler sings *tenna-tenna see see seee*, as I was taught as a child. But the bird was named after the state of Tennessee neither for its song nor because it nests there (except for New England, all of its breeding range is near or north of the Canadian border, and it winters in the tropics), but because it first became known to science from a migrant bird shot in that state. Its song has also been rendered *tika tika tika tika, swit swit, sit-sit-sti-sit-sit-sit* or *sidit-sidit-sidit-sidit-swit-swit-sit-sit-sit-sit-sit-sit*. There is variation from one bird to another, and it really says neither *tika* nor *sidit*, nor, for that matter, *tenna*. All are attempts to render the song into print to provide a rhythmic and somewhat pitch-indicative mnemonic.

The Nashville Warbler (which is no more accurately named, having first become known to science from a migrant collected in that city) is said to sing *see-pit see-pit see-pit see-pit titititi*. One might be forgiven for not quite understanding the differences between *tika, sidit,* and *see-pit,* and yet those descriptions work well for me if—and only if—I'm familiar with the song or I can compare the printed, made-up words to a bird I hear singing.

Though there are variations in the songs of any oscines, a written attempt to describe similar songs of birds can work. There is a thin, trill-like component at the end of the Nashville's song that is faster, containing slightly less distinct notes than a similar ending to the typical song of a Tennessee Warbler. Knowing that, a listener can more easily learn to distinguish between the two species.

By far the best way to learn bird songs is to go into the field during the breeding season with an expert who knows the sounds and can help you learn them. The second best method is to make use of tapes, compact disks, and CD ROMs that feature birdsongs and calls. Musical notations and sonograms work, at least to some degree, for those birders who have made the effort to learn to read them, but most have not done so.

Peabody Bird

On average, I receive at least one or two phone calls each summer from people who, upon visiting the north woods to canoe, camp, or spend time at a cottage, have heard a distinctive birdsong over and over again. Sometimes the bird would sing at night. What is it? As soon as they say that it ends in long, clear notes, I know the bird they mean. In a very old American bird book, a naturalist named George Gladden had this to say about the singing of this particular species: "It is night, very still, very dark. The subdued murmur of the forest ebbs and flows with the voices of the furtive folk, an undertone fearful to break the night calm. Suddenly across the dusk of silence flashes a single thread of silver, vibrating, trembling with some unguessed ecstasy of emotion. 'Ah! poor Canada, Canada, Canada' it mourns passionately, and falls silent. That is all."

Where it bred and sang in the New England states, the bird in question used to be called the Peabody Bird, as it allegedly sang *Ol' Sam Peabody Peabody Peabody.* North of the border, it was called the Canada Bird. It was also known as the Peverly Bird, having sung the song to a farmer named Peverly, who was trying to decide if he should plant his crop when he heard a bird sing *Sow wheat, Peverly Peverly, Peverly!* Upon following the bird's advice, he eventually had a successful harvest, or so the old legend goes.

The species in question is the White-throated Sparrow, and to my ears it says nothing about Peabody, Peverly, or Canada, but does normally end its song with three clear, distinctive notes. These are nearly pure tones (sine waves), more like a pure whistle, and have little or no overtones (harmonics) or glottal stops that would actually suggest consonant sounds to the human ear. Trying to render pure, or nearly pure, tones as words, presumably in the interest of helping one remember what bird sings what song, is far more fanciful than using words that represent more slurred sounds that are rich in harmonics, such as the *phee-beeeee* song of the Eastern Phoebe, a common breeding bird throughout much of eastern and central North America.

Onomatopoeic Nomenclature

The Hoopoe is a bird native to Europe, Asia, and Africa. It is, like the Eastern Phoebe mentioned above, onomatopoeically named, meaning it is named in phonetic imitation of its voice. The call of the Hoopoe in breeding season is a low, soft, but far-carrying *hoop-hoop-hoop*. The bird gives the impression of working hard at the production of the call, distending its neck and bowing as it *hoops*. The Hoopoe can also meow like a kitten or utter a low *caa-caa-caa-caa*.

Found throughout much of North America, the Killdeer is an elegantly patterned plover that often frequents schoolyards, dumps, shorelines, farm fields, sand quarries, and anywhere else that is flat and lightly vegetated. But why on earth was it called a Killdeer? The name is onomatopoeic, but does a Killdeer really say *kill deer?* Various sources give a number of descriptions and phonetic renderings of the Killdeer's plaintive and familiar call, usually along the lines of *kill-dee* or *dee-dee-dee* or something similar. The call can be quite shrill. While it may seem to urge the assassination of a *dee,* a *deee,* or a *deeah,* this pert bird does not seem to be urging the slaughter of any species of deer.

Such phonetics, in combination with a description of various features of the call—and taking into consideration the bird's range, habitat, behavior, and other factors—are the best way of identifying bird calls and songs as to species, other than by comparing them to a recording or having someone who knows tell you what they are.

The Whip-poor-will

When heard singing in the summer night, the Whip-poor-will, native to much of North America, really does seem to be saying, *WHIP-poor-WILL.* It is a loud, clear song repeated over and over. In an old sketchbook, I used the following notation for a bird singing from very nearby: *ch-wh-WHIP-pr'-per-wiill.* I was struggling to get just as close to every nuance of the sound as I could, and included a curving squiggle over the end word to indicate that the call's final note tended to be upslurred. Such efforts at phonetic imitation must be limited, of course, but they are successful if they allow a hearer to identify the species. I would think that no one could read the above descriptions of either the Killdeer or the Whip-poor-will and, if standing in the right place at the right time, fail to identify either species by sound alone. However, use of mnemonics tends to be quite subjective, and there are no doubt folks who have heard both Killdeers and

Whip-poor-wills without ever thinking their calls resembled anything like the words "kill deer" or "Whip poor Will."

The Whip-poor-will is a member of the family of birds that includes nighthawks and nightjars, the Caprimulgidae, and is native to North America. Like most (presumably all, although vocalizations of some are little known, or completely unknown) members of the family, it has a number of vocalizations that are less distinctive than the mating song. There are several subspecies, and some of the calls may be specific to a given race. Even the *Whip-poor-Will* call varies geographically, with southwestern birds having less sharply defined articulation and the strongest emphasis on the concluding syllable, in distinction from the eastern birds, where the emphasis is more on the first and last syllables.

Throughout its wide range, the call of the Whip-poor-will is generally well known to rural folks. However, a great many people have heard it for every one who has actually seen the bird. The species is nocturnal. During the day it sits quietly, its remarkably cryptic color and pattern blending in to a matrix of dead leaves and forest floor debris. Sometimes it sits on a branch lengthwise, looking more like a knot or bit of loose bark than a bird. One of the best ways to see a Whip-poor-will is to drive rural roads at night, looking for the ruby-toned reflected eye-shine of the birds as they sit on the edge of the road or on low branches or fences to the side of the road. A high-powered spotlight helps, but using such a device puts one at risk of being suspected by law officials as a poacher jacklighting deer.

Looking like a large, buffier version of the Whip-poor-will is the closely related, onomatopoeically named Chuck-will's-widow. The bird breeds throughout most of the eastern United States and winters from the southeastern United States as far south as northern South America. This species also has a three-syllable call, delivered emphatically, but sounding more like *CHUCK-will-wilyo*, at least to my ear. The Chuck-will's-widow's distribution and habitat overlap those of the Whip-poor-will, although the breeding range of the latter species extends much farther north (Manitoba, north-central Ontario, Quebec, New Brunswick, and New England), southwest (California to western Texas), and south (Honduras and El Salvador).

The Bobwhites

The Common, or Northern, Bobwhite is a species of New World quail (Odontophoridae) found throughout much of the eastern United States, with various subspecies, some quite different in their markings, occurring as far south as southern Mexico and parts of Cuba and the Isle of Pines, although it has been widely introduced elsewhere. It almost says its name. To my ear, the call is *b-ba-WHITE,* all clearly whistled with the last note upslurred. The tracheal syrinxes of the quails are structurally quite simple, but the Common Bobwhite, a familiar and well-studied species, has ten to twenty-four distinct calls. Those old enough to remember the golden age of radio in America might remember the Common Bobwhite's call being used in Rinso White radio commercials. The bird's call, to the admen, sounded like *rin-so-WHITE.*

While the name bobwhite was first applied to birds from the eastern United States, very similar vocalizations seem to be common to other members of the genus. These are the Black-throated, or Yucatan, Bobwhite of the Yucatan Peninsula; the Spot-bellied Bobwhite of southern Mexico and Central America; and the Crested Bobwhite of Panama and northern South America. The Crested is sometimes considered to be the same species as the Spot-bellied. A Black-throated Bobwhite may not look much like a Common Bobwhite, but hearing its call from a thicket in northern Belize, one can easily recognize the call as that of a bobwhite, albeit one with something of an accent. Even within the Northern Bobwhite species there is so much variation in color and pattern that appearance may be considered more variable than voice.

This genus appears to be rapidly evolving, with approximately forty-five different subspecies recognized among the four species. Each of those subspecies would vary at least to some degree in terms of voice or appearance, and yet the "bobwhite" call is consistently recognizable throughout all of them.

The Saw-whet Owl

There is a small, rotund species of owl in North America that is known as the Northern Saw-whet Owl. It is named for its voice, which sounds like a saw being whetted, or sharpened. Actually, the most often heard call is a monotonous, single, clear whistle, uttered about twice per second. It also has a rasping call note that reminded someone of a saw being sharpened on a stone, no doubt a familiar sound back in the nineteenth century, but less likely to evoke a memory of such sound in the contemporary listener.

Numerous other birds are named for their calls or songs. A partial list of North American species includes the Clapper Rail (clapping vocalization); Piping Plover (vocal call); Willet (onomatopoeic); Plain Chachalaca (onomatopoeic); Wandering Tattler (call sounds like someone tattling); the godwits (onomatopoeic); the curlews (onomatopoeic); Laughing Gull (call

sounds like human laughter); Mew Gull (a mewing cry); Common Pauraque (onomatopoeic); Common Poor-will (onomatopoeic); the phoebes (onomatopoeic); the chickadees (onomatopoeic); Gray Catbird (mews like a cat); Veery (onomatopoeic); the towhees (onomatopoeic); the pipits (onomatopoeic, although not all pipits in this large family give vocalizations that fit the name); Warbling Vireo (its song could be called warbling); Grasshopper Sparrow (makes a grasshopperlike, buzzing trill); Vesper Sparrow (sings in the evening, as though singing its vespers); Song Sparrow (has a wondrously rich and distinctive song); Dickcissel (onomatopoeic); Lark Sparrow, Lark Bunting, and meadowlarks (larklike singing, especially to someone unfamiliar with actual lark singing); and Chipping Sparrow (frequently heard call note is a short, dry chip; however, the song is a trill, and Trilling Sparrow would be an equally appropriate name).

The New World wood warblers are an interesting exception. It is often commented that they actually don't warble. In fact, the birds were first called warblers in the belief that they were closely related to the warblers of Europe, at least some of which earned the epithet honestly—they really do warble. The similarities that led to that conclusion, based mostly on shape and size, proved to be superficial, however, and the birds of the Americas were called wood warblers, or New World warblers, while their namesakes are generally referred to as Old World warblers. These changes are not completely successful in avoiding confusion. There is an Old World warbler known as the Wood Warbler, which really could be said to warble, and not all so-called Old World warblers are confined to the Old World.

The Northern Saw-whet Owl gets its name from one of its calls, a rasping sound like that made when a saw is "whetted" or sharpened.

TEN

Bill Rattling, Clattering, and Snapping

Deep inside the songbird, lungs and air sacs control the flow of air that produces vocalization. The sound begins within the body, and the last part of the bird that can influence the quality of the sound is the beak. But for some birds, the beak is the beginning and end of sound production. This is especially true of a group of birds that are noteworthy for poorly developed voices—indeed, some may have virtually no voice at all—the storks. Storks tend to have long, stout beaks, which effectively replace the need for elaborate vocal anatomy.

It is not true, as some people believe, that storks are entirely mute. However, their voices do tend to be among the least complex and least obvious of all birds, essentially consisting of hisses, cronks, croaks, weak whistles, grunts, moos, and guttural gasps. Storks' beaks range from slender to massive and serve to augment impoverished vocal repertoires with various degrees of bill clattering, rattling, or snapping.

The most developed bill clattering among stork species is practiced by one of the more weaker-voiced, the Eurasian White Stork, the same species famed for nesting on chimneys in quaint European villages and fabled to deliver bundles of joy to expectant human mothers.

In *The Handbook of British Birds*, Vol. 3 (H. F. & G. Witherby Ltd., 1943), edited by H. F. Witherby, the Eurasian White Stork's bill-clattering display is described thus:

'Bill clattering' is a rapid rhythmical clapping of mandibles, producing a loud almost trilling sound with peculiar modulations of pace and pitch. It is usually accompanied by singular movements, neck being curved backwards till crown touches back, then brought forward and downward again, then back; throat-pouch acts as resonator. . . . [Bill rattling is] essentially expression of excitement and not only functions as greeting-ceremony at nest, but may be performed by one bird or by both when they have been some time together, or on approach of a hostile Stork. Young clatter feebly as soon as hatched. In defensive or threatening posture . . . wings are drooped, tail fanned and cocked up, neck somewhat extended, with bill pointing down and throat-sac swollen. Coition on nest, male springing to female's back, adjusting balance by flapping movement of wings, then bending legs and lowering himself into requisite position with wings still spread and moving; at same time makes gentle clapping noises with bill amongst neck feathers of female, whose head is drawn back so that the crown rests against male's breast and bill touches his with gentle rubbing movement.

The Eurasian White Stork is the world's maestro of bill rattling. At the other extreme is the Saddle-billed Stork, which does not appear to engage in bill rattling and, upon maturity, apparently really is voiceless.

The most vocal of the storks is a scavenger, the Marabou, native to Africa. It is also a noisy bill rattler. Baby Marabous will sometimes make a clumsy attempt at bill rattling. Although bill rattling is used in breeding displays, it is also used by the Marabou as part of a threat activity.

Typical of scavenger species, the Marabou must compete with others for the carrion it consumes. Hungry vultures, ravens, and jackals may gather at a carcass, along with the Marabous. A Marabou's towering stature and aggressive bill rattling may help compensate for lack of fangs and long claws, although having the ability to fly has its own survival value when a lion decides to return to the kill.

The Marabou's vocalizations have been described as "impossible to syllablize in any known language." That has not kept the authors of bird

The Marabou, a stork native to Africa, has a massive beak which can be rattled to intimidate other animals.

guides from making the effort. In *Birds of Kenya and Northern Tanzania,* by Dale A. Zimmerman, Donald A. Turner, and David J. Pearson (Princeton University Press, 1996), the authors say, with reference to the species: "Usually silent apart from bill-clattering and loud wheezy whine of air across flight feathers in low flight, but moans, moos and squeals at the nest; courting bird gives a repeated hoarse whinnying, *wu-wuwuwuwuwuwuwuwuwuwa-ekk.*"

Bill Rattling and Snapping in Other Species
Storks are not the only birds that rattle or clack their beaks to make noise. Ground hornbills are nearly turkey-size birds that strut about the plains of much of Africa. A mated pair of Northern Ground Hornbills will slap each other's beaks. The loud clacking sound thus produced is purely a mechanical noise. Their vocalizations include a deep grunting noise that sounds similar to the noise made by an African lion.

Cassowaries, the sole members of the family Casuariidae, which is restricted to rain forests of northern Australia and New Guinea, are huge, flightless birds that clack their bills, whistle, and produce a variety of rumbles, hisses, loud roars, and low hoots. The reasons for most of these vocalizations are not yet well understood, but bill clacking, hissing, and whistling are clearly meant to be threatening. The threat is not idle; the bird's kick has been known to disembowel a human.

The albatross family includes the species of birds with the greatest wingspread, the Wandering Albatross, and the related Royal Albatross, whose wingspread is approximately 3.5 meters. Albatrosses, particularly on their breeding grounds, have a variety of most unmusical sounds that can make a nesting colony quite a noisy place. All species have a castanet-type rattling sound produced by rapid bill clattering. It seems to serve both as part of the courtship ritual and, in a different context, as a threat display to other albatrosses. Sometimes, particularly early in the breeding system, brief but aggressive skirmishes break out. Elaborate visual displays, which involve spreading their great wings and shuffling about as they point their beaks skyward, are further means of establishing territory.

Several species of herons include bill snapping or castanet-type bill rattling in their noise repertoires. A familiar example is the Black-crowned Night Heron. Snapping its stout beak is part of a suite of breeding displays. The bird is found in North and South America, Eurasia, Africa, and Indochina. It is a common species in many regions, and sometimes nesting colonies are close to human habitation. Indeed, one of the easiest places in the United States to watch and hear these birds display is the National Zoo in Washington, D.C. They are not caged birds, but wild ones that, each year, nest in the trees that shade the bird house and ponds near the entrance to the park.

Although the aberrant Boat-billed Heron, native to Central and South America, is similar in size, shape, and color to the Black-crowned Night Heron, it is really very different from other herons. Unlike all other herons, the Boat-billed has a very broad, flattened beak that is employed in producing a distinctive popping sound. The loud pop is often accompanied by a brief note—*an.*

Bill Clacking in Owls

"Watch out for the owl," my mother said. We were standing in our small living room. A guest, drink in hand, was telling a story, with much gesticulating. He looked at my mother and where she was pointing, nodded, and kept talking, arms flailing for emphasis. I was a kid and frankly was surprised that he failed to heed my mother's warning. She repeated it. The man shrugged, looked at the owl perched on the corner of the television set, and continued talking and waving his arms around.

Suddenly the owl dropped his head and fanned his wings and began snapping his beak. Our houseguest leaped back, spilling the drink and swearing. "It's ALIVE!" he wailed.

Our mistake. It didn't occur to us that he thought we would have a stuffed owl perched on our TV. Our house was always full of quite live birds, and a Long-eared Owl in the living room, while a bit unusual, was not unheard of. It was a wild bird, unafraid of people, as is so often the case with owls, and we had simply been allowing him the freedom of the room when our guest happened to arrive.

When it feels threatened and trapped, a Long-eared Owl will lower its head and spread its wings at right angles to the body, tilting them so they present, from the front, a view of their dorsal surfaces. The inner edges of the wings meet over the owl's back. The breast feathers are spread below, and the face, with its conspicuous forward-facing eyes, is in the middle. The bird shuffles from one foot to the other and loudly clacks its beak. The owl on the TV was not afraid of people, but our friend's arm waving finally triggered its defensive response, which certainly had a strong effect on our guest.

The principle behind the wing spreading is similar to that of suddenly opening an umbrella in the face of a charging dog—it creates a sudden

Barry Kent MacKay

increase in the size of the object, thus breaking the concentrated focus of the attacker. The clacking is a further threat.

All owl species I've handled have clacked their beaks. Bill clacking when stressed is a reaction often accompanied by hissing. If you put your finger into the bird's mouth, it rarely bites down, and as long as the beak's hooked tip is not pressing into flesh at a right angle, even if the bird does bite, the effect is rather innocuous. The owl's real defensive capability lies in the talons. The sharp claws of even the medium-size Long-eared Owl can draw blood. The talons of a Great Horned Owl or a Eurasian Eagle Owl can cause more serious injury.

Even a nestling owl will go into this defensive bill-clacking display on sight of something unexpected, like a curious human. Whatever the effect on other species, the young owl's attempt at looking fierce usually elicits a smile from a human observer, especially one who likes owls.

Bill Clapping and Snapping in Passerines

I've also become the object of stress-induced bill clapping when handling certain passerines. At least some species of tyrant flycatchers, which usually have broad bills and bright mouth linings, will snap their beaks when being handled.

Eastern Kingbirds, which are tyrant flycatchers native to North America, are one of many small bird species particularly noted for their fierce attacks on larger birds, such as crows, herons, and hawks. In bravura aerial performances, the kingbirds will swoop down on the much larger bird, even to the point of striking it from above. The kingbirds scream a thin call and rapidly snap their beaks, flashing yellow mouth linings. It's all bluff; there is no power in their bites. The observer can also hear the audible snap of even a small flycatcher's beak as it captures a nearby flying insect. American Robins, Gray Catbirds, and various other oscine species will sometimes bill snap when handled.

Baby Hoopoes, a nonpasserine species, will, when disturbed in the nest, snap their slender bills in alarm.

With its broad bill, so unlike the bills of other herons, the Boat-billed Heron makes an odd popping sound. This mostly nocturnal species is native to Central and South America.

ELEVEN

Honkers, Quackers, Whistlers, Whoopers, and Screamers: The Waterfowl

If it looks like a duck and it quacks like a duck, it may be a duck, but the converse does not necessarily hold true. Although most ducks are more or less identifiable by appearance, relatively few of the many duck species go *quack*.

One that does is also one of the most widespread and best known of all bird species, the Mallard. Mallards are found throughout most of North America, including Alaska and Mexico, Greenland, much of Eurasia, and North Africa, with introduced populations in parts of the Southern Hemisphere.

Mallards

The *quack* call of the wild Mallard, and several closely related species, is a contact call given by the female. Typically, the bird utters a series of *quacks* of various intensities and frequencies, usually trailing off toward the end of the series, along the lines of *qu-QUACK, quack, quack quack, quack*. Often any one series of quacks is superimposed over similar calls from nearby hen Mallards so that they overlap and blend into a gabbling sound. The mating call of the male mallard is a soft, reedy *kreeep* or a low *kreb, kreeb,* or *qwek*.

Contact calling is important and frequent among waterfowl of a great many species. Sport hunters can lure many species within range by combining the visual stimulus of artificial decoys that are often rather crude approximations of the real thing with rather unrefined imitations of the female birds' contact calls. Ducks find the higher fidelity of recorded calls much more irresistible, thus the use of such recordings by sport hunters is banned, as it would be too easy to destroy too many birds.

Compared with those of songbirds, the calls of ducks are limited in variability. However, variation does occur and can be inherited. One domesticated breed of Mallard, called the Aylesbury Duck, has been selectively bred to produce a very different male call, more of a grunt.

All Mallard-type ducks are closely related and sound pretty much the same, although the Hawaiian Duck, presumably because of its small size, has a slightly higher-pitched voice and the female Laysan Duck tends to be quieter. Both species are confined to the Hawaiian Islands.

Swans

Because of the noise it makes with its wings, the species of swan most widely distributed in North America was once known as the Whistling Swan. It is now called the Tundra Swan. This pure white bird has a far-carrying ululation that, when uttered by hundreds or thousands of voices at once, can make a significant impression on the human listener. As its name implies, the species tends to nest in the northern tundra, but it is a common migrant through the Great Lakes and in the Prairies, wintering, often in large numbers, mostly in the Central Valley of California, but also along the Atlantic coast from Maryland to North Carolina and in some inland areas. It is now considered to be a race of the same species as the Bewick's Swan, which breeds in the far-northern reaches of Eurasia.

The Trumpeter Swan, whose bugling call is stronger than that of the Tundra, is a slightly larger bird. Closely related to both, and as large as the Trumpeter, is the Old World Whooper Swan. Both species have powerful voices and are the largest species of waterfowl in the world.

Swans' vocal quality owes much to a swelling at the base of the trachea that acts as a resonating chamber amplifying the great birds' spectacular calls. This expanded sound chamber is called the *bulla* (plural *bullae*) and is part of the syrinx. It is bony, usually asymmetrical, and found only in the male. It probably has more to do with altering the nature of the call than with the power of the call.

There is another adaptation in the more loudly voiced swans that enhances sound production. The trachea loops through the interior of the breastbone, or sternum. This greatly increases the volume of air forced up through the trachea, providing a deep resonance from the very depths of the bird's large body.

A similar, even more convoluted coiling of the elongated trachea is found in cranes. In fact, the entire trachea of a Whooping Crane, when uncoiled, measures some 58 inches, or about the length of the bird itself, with about 24 of those inches coiled in a supporting hollow chamber in the sternum. A Whooping Crane's voice can carry up to 3 miles. The Trumpeter Swan's voice is not quite so loud but probably can reach a similar distance under ideal conditions. The pitch of the male swan's call is usually lower than the female's. The pitch of the male goose's call tends to be higher than that of the female.

In sharp contrast to the vocalization of other northern swan species, the Mute Swan is relatively quiet. However, the birds have snorting and grunting sounds, as well as the hissing that is familiar to anyone who has ever strayed close to a Mute Swan's nest and been challenged by protective parents. The Mute Swan practices none of the far-carrying, resonant calling associated with other swan species of the Northern Hemisphere.

> ### The Legend of the Swan Song
>
> There is a tradition that a dying swan utters one last, beautiful song. It does not happen often, but it has been noted. One possible explanation is that upon being struck by shotgun pellets, a pellet may puncture the trachea. As the bird expires and its muscles relax, air within the bird's convoluted internal trachea and respiratory system expels through the opening, producing the single long, sadly musical note that has been heard by a very few people. Swans mate for life, or until one partner is lost, and sometimes a bird will keep company with its fallen mate, adding to the poignancy of the tale. Swan hunting is legal in several U.S. states, but most swan species are protected wherever they occur. ■

The Mute Swan is native to Eurasia but has established a large, self-sustaining population in eastern North America. This is the species, with its orange beak and habit of fanning its inner wing feathers into "sails," that is most often seen in parks, zoos, and on private estates.

Whistling-ducks

Whistling-ducks used to be called tree-ducks because they perched in trees. Though the species found in North America may sit in trees, overall

The lovely Mute Swan, native to Europe and Asia, is not really mute, but can utter a hissing sound during its threat display.

they are not particularly arboreal, and some non–North American species have little or no affinity for trees. Something else that connected this homogenous assembly of waterfowl species is that these ducks do a lot of whistling. You'll see them called tree-ducks in older bird books, but generally they are now called whistling-ducks.

The eight species of whistling-ducks are scattered in a broad band that extends around the middle of the planet, incorporating the tropics and subtropics and extending into warm temperate latitudes as far south as southern Australia and as far north as the Atlantic coastal plain of the southeastern United States.

Physically, all whistling-ducks are short-tailed, long-legged, and long-necked. Their beaks are long and elegantly tapered. Males and females are nearly identical in color and pattern. The birds stand more upright than Mallards and most other duck species. In flight, the tips of the feet extend beyond the tail. All species have at least some tawny-buff or rufous-brown coloring to their plumage. They are usually quite gregarious, frequently appearing in noisy flocks. Often they are nocturnal, their shrill voices betraying their presence in dark, tropical wetlands.

Most whistling-duck species utter shrill whistling noises, quite unducklike, if ducklike is judged to be the Mallard's *quack*. The wings usually make a dull throbbing or, in some species, a whistling sound, in flight. The birds usually call from the water, while perched, or while in flight.

The Fulvous Whistling-Duck is one of the most widely distributed of any birds, being found on four continents: North America, South America, Africa, and Asia. What may be even more interesting than the huge extent of its range is the fact that the bird remains the same throughout, with no subspeciation and no regional dialects or other variations in calls. A Fulvous Whistling-Duck in coastal South Carolina sounds like one in India or Madagascar or northern Argentina. The call is a loud squeal, *per-chweeee.*

The very beautiful White-faced Whistling-Duck is found in southern Central and South America, and in tropical and southern Africa. It, too, is very vocal, with a three-note whistle, the last note held the longest. Under stress, the bird utters a *wheee* call. It also shows no geographic variation in appearance or voice throughout its disjunct range.

The West Indian Whistling-Duck, also called Black-billed or Cuban, is confined to parts of the West Indies, where it is much rarer than it used to be and may be considered a threatened or endangered species. True to both the former English name of West Indian Tree Duck and its scientific name, *Dendrocygna arborea,* this bird spends a lot of time perched in trees, even in tall palms, where it consumes fruit, as does a trogon or tanager. It is often nocturnal while feeding and is less vocal than most other whistling-ducks, although it, too, utters a shrill whistled note.

The Lesser Whistling-Duck is found through much of southern Asia. It is the smallest of the whistling-ducks and quite abundant. These ducks whistle constantly, uttering a clear, low whistle, particularly while they are in flight. The beating wings produce their own whistling sound, as is true of many duck species. The Lesser Whistling-Duck also has a low, rather *quack*-like contact note.

The relatively little-studied Spotted Whistling-Duck has a fairly extensive range in the East Indies and New Guinea. The Spotted is one of the less vocal of the group, although the birds do exchange low, whistled notes and sometimes utter harsh notes. Their wings make a distinctive whirring sound.

The Plumed, Eyton's, Red-legged, or Grass Whistling-Duck is a grassland species from tropical Australia. Flocks are incessantly atwitter, whether at rest, grazing, or in flight. The call is a high, whistled *what-chew*. The feathers of the flank are modified into elongated plumes that are pale yellow and black and tend to stick out to the sides of the wings when the bird is perched or on the water.

From the same general region comes the Wandering Whistling-Duck of northern Australia and the East Indies. It is another of the twittering ducks, with a call that is a weaker version of that of the Plumed Whistling-Duck.

The first species of whistling-duck I ever saw in the wild is the very handsome Black-bellied Whistling-Duck, found from the southern Texas–Mexico border south through much of Central America, as far south as Argentina. The birds are noisy, uttering a high-pitched call consisting of four notes, often given during flight. The species is relatively arboreal and nocturnal.

Magpie Geese

In addition to being the native land of the world's only black swan, Australia is home to many other odd birds, including the strange-looking Magpie Goose. It is unclear if this bird is more closely related to geese or swans, or perhaps neither. In a sense, it's a link to another family, the screamers of South America. Magpie relates to highly distinctive plumage. It has a black head and neck and a white body with much black on the wings and thighs or tibia just above the heel, where the leg joins the body, and a black tail. The pattern bears superficial resemblance not only to the boldly patterned Black-billed Magpie of the Northern Hemisphere (but not Australia) but also, to a much lesser degree, to the Australian Magpie, another bird found only in Australia, and conspicuous by virtue of both black and white patterning and loud, flutelike calls.

Magpie Geese are long-necked, gooselike birds with a knobby crest on the head and a long, tapered pink and gray beak. The feet are big and yellow, and the toes are only webbed at the base, facilitating perching on limbs and branches. This is, in short, a very peculiar looking goose—or duck.

The birds have a gooselike honking call that has a galvanizing effect on other Magpie Geese. Both sexes call, and the honk of the male is typically answered by honking from several females. Although the birds apparently mate for life, one male may have two mates, who peacefully share the same nest. Large family groups assemble in wetlands, joining with other family groups in cacophonous flocks.

The Screamers

The order Anseriformes is divided into two suborders, the Anseres, which contains the single family Anatidae—the ducks, geese, and swans—and the Anhimae, which contains a single family also, the Anhimidae, more popularly known as the screamers. There are well over 150 species of Anatids, but only three species of screamers, all native to South America.

Screamers are birds of wetlands and open grasslands, quite able to swim, sitting high in the water. However, they are not inclined to take to the water, nor are they known to dive underwater. They readily sit on branches. Screamers are large, goose- or turkey-size birds with very long legs and long toes that are webbed only at the bases. A sharp spur sticks out from the wrist, a characteristic they share with the Spur-winged Goose of Africa. These weapons seem to be used in intraspecific disputes, as the horny sheath of the wing spur has been found imbedded in the breasts of other screamers. The plumage is generally gray or black, with white markings.

Screamers do scream, deafeningly, for hours on end. Their loud, unmusical, atonal voices carry well, being heard as far as 2 miles. One bird calling serves to trigger others to call. Males and females may duet for hours. The sound is not usually appreciated by human listeners subjected to hearing it for lengthy periods of time. The appearance of a predator may spark a series of screams that warns away potential prey. Sometimes the birds scream while flying; in fact, a whole flock of birds circling overhead may contribute to the ruckus.

Screamers sometimes make a booming or crackling noise. This probably occurs as a result of a complex network of air sacs that are underneath the skin. These air sacs, in conjunction with highly pneumatic bones, account for the birds being highly buoyant on those rare occasions when they do swim. But apparently the bird has the ability to abruptly contract surrounding musculature and collapse the air sacs, thus mechanically creating a sudden drumming or crackling sound that appears to serve as a threat to nearby antagonists.

TWELVE

Galliformes:
Grouse, Pheasants,
and Related Birds

Grouse (Family Tetraonidae)

Grouse are restricted to the Northern Hemisphere. The best-known North
American species is the widely distributed Ruffed Grouse. Sage Grouse,
Sharp-tailed Grouse, prairie-chickens, and ptarmigan are other grouse
species. Ptarmigan, small, noisy grouse that mostly live above the tree
lines of arctic, subarctic, and alpine regions, are white in winter and mottled brown in summer. In the United Kingdom, however, the Willow
Ptarmigan maintains a richly red-brown (male) or brown (female) mottled
color year-round and is known as the Red Grouse. Eurasion Black Grouse
and Western Capercaillie are other well-known Eurasian grouse species.

Sage Grouse

In late winter, the mature male Sage Grouse gather on the lek prior to
dawn. They are few in numbers and hesitant, at first, then they gather in
increasing numbers each day to act out a remarkable pageant. The lek is
an area of trodden-down vegetation and earth. One lek site might serve for
many generations.

Enlarged, white, pendulous sacs hang around the necks of the males,
like horse collars. The sacs are inflated with air during the display, while
the birds' long, spike-shaped tail feathers are fanned and the soft undertail
coverts fluffed. The wings are stiffly drooped down and forward, and the

birds scurry about with short, little mincing steps. In an apparent eruption of passion, they stroke the floppy sacs with the outer primary feathers of their wings, making a brisk, brushing noise against modified feathers on the sides of the inflated sacs. The sound does not carry far. At this impassioned moment, sprays of slender plumes stick up from the tops of their heads. Above their eyes are yellow wattles that are swollen like a clown's fake eyebrows. As the birds pump their heads and the sacs quiver, a round yellow patch of skin, looking a little like the yolk of a frying egg, emerges briefly on either side of the breast, and there is a loud *pop*.

The pendulous sacs that the male Sage Grouse inflates are being pushed out by air filling the esophageal air sac, within the neck. Sexual selection over many generations has led to the sac being modified to allow the inflation beneath the skin that produces the spectacular display. Pushed from within, the sac is heaved upward and allowed to collapse, and then heaved upward again as it fills with air. The quivering, elastic walls of the sac expand to hold approximately 4 liters of air. The superficial muscles of the chest are then abruptly contracted and the air released with a loud *pop*. It takes only three frenzied seconds for the grouse to go through the cycle of filling the sac with air and then releasing it, the action accompanied by the brisk rubbing of the sides of the sac with the stiff primary wing feathers. The quick run, or strut, of the male, along with the stroking of the air sac, gives the appearance of exciting the male into a brief build-up of tension that climaxes in the explosive release of pent-up air. It is an elaborate visual and audio display.

Other Grouse

All grouse have well-developed vocal capability, and some create low-frequency sounds that derive from special adaptations of the trachea and the pharynx, at the upper end of the trachea. The prairie-chickens produce booming sounds that carry across the plains. The Eurasian Black Grouse has a loud *rookooing* call that a human ear can detect at a distance of some 3 or 4 kilometers. The Western Capercaillie, a grouse nearly as large as the Sage Grouse, has no external display of air sacs, even though they are employed in sound production. In the capercaillie, there is a loop in the trachea that increases its length by one-third. As with the Sage Grouse, the capercaillie can increase the volume employed in sound production through swelling of the air sacs of the throat and neck, giving the bird a thick-necked look as he calls.

The Western Capercaillie's vocalizations are very much a part of the rural folklore of northern Europe. German hunters have told me that the bird is deaf when calling, and thus can be approached only while it is engaged in its distinctive breeding display. Within a brief period, about ten seconds, the capercaillie makes a tapping sound, "reminiscent of water dripping or of sticks being knocked together," which is followed by a "drum roll" of rapidly uttered metallic-sounding notes whose frequency of utterance accelerates until merging, followed by an explosive *pop,* and concluding with a "type of rhythmic rasping and unmusical panting" known as *whetting,* as described in the *Handbook of the Birds of the World* (1994).

Within the species, there are numerous subspecies—about a dozen are usually described. The white-bellied birds from central Siberia and northwestern Mongolia lack the *pop* component of the breeding vocalizations. A closely related species, the Black-billed Capercaillie, is found in eastern Siberia.

While it might seem that the elaborate combination of distinctive visual and audio performances would be enough to clearly distinguish the performing male of each grouse species, in fact, hybridization among members of the family does occur. This may lead to offspring unable to successfully breed with either parent species. A significant exception is the hybrid between the Sharp-tailed Grouse and Greater Prairie-chicken. Both are lek species and both perform displays that involve bowing and inflated neck sacs. Their displays apparently are similar enough to lead to some hybridizing, producing fertile offspring that backcross to create a range of mixed characteristics.

Although the Blue Grouse, of the mountains of western North America, does not have a lek display, the male swells the air sacs of the neck, and at the height of the breeding display, they show as round, yellow sacs on either side of the neck.

As a generality, species that do not form pair bonds are more predisposed to hybridization than those that do. Lek species with intense displays, be they hummingbirds or grouse, fit this model. Nevertheless, hybrids also occur among species that do form pair bonds. One obvious reason is that the two forms have not been separated long enough to develop adequate isolating mechanisms. In North America, it seems likely that the last ice age divided the progenitor of the Baltimore and Bullock's Orioles into two separate populations, each evolving changes in color,

The pointed tail feathers that give the Sharp-tailed Grouse its name are audibly rattled during the enthusiastic breeding display, performed on the high plains and prairies of North America.

song, and other characteristics. But the isolation did not last long enough, and where their breeding ranges overlap, hybridization does occur.

During the breeding display of the prairie-chickens and the Blue Grouse, there are several things that happen within the birds' bodies to block air from escaping until the right moment. Air cannot escape when, with the beak closed, the tongue is raised to block the opening, at the roof of the mouth, that leads to the nostrils. Simultaneously, the glottis, which is the opening at the top of the trachea, is placed at the opening of the esophagus. Thus the esophagus, which leads to the stomach, fills with air from the trachea, which in turn takes air from lungs and those air sacs that are not modified into sound production organs. This greatly increases the volume of air that ultimately is available to make some quite loud sounds.

The syrinx, while less complex than that of songbirds, nevertheless also serves some function in vocalizations in grouse and other Galliformes. The Hazel Grouse, native to Europe and Asia, is capable of producing a high, whistled song that resembles that of a songbird. Most other grouse vocalizations, apart from the booming, popping, *rookooing,* and other sounds associated with highly visual mating displays, are of a clucking, cackling, or grunting nature, lacking anything approaching the complexity and variety of songbirds' songs.

Drumming and Other Mechanical Sounds

Familiar to many who visit woodlots and forests throughout much of North America, particularly in the spring, is a very low, dull, and muffled throbbing, slow at first and then speeding up, like a piston engine coming to life—the drumming of the Ruffed Grouse.

Although the drumming is heard far more often than seen, one can watch the actual display by finding the drumming log that the bird perches upon and setting up a blind nearby. The bird stands rather upright, his wide tail spread and held stiffly against the log or stump during the actual drumming. The dark band of feathers around the neck, just below the head, may be spread into a face-framing ruff when the bird, wings held stiffly and tail fanned, struts before a prospective mate. The ruff may be relaxed during the five to ten or more seconds when the bird is actually drumming. What can be seen with the naked eye is that the wings are rapidly beaten in front of the bird. One beat and then another and another occur in rapid acceleration, until the wings are a furious blur of motion. Each beat produces a low, muffled, drumlike sound that carries far through the woods. The first few beats are distinct but quickly reach a crescendo in which they run together and then abruptly stop.

The question that used to plague naturalists was how the bird does it. The wings move too quickly for the human eye to catch the details; however, that did not stop speculation. For most observers, the question was whether the bird's wings produced the sound by hitting each other like hands clapping, by hitting the sides of the bird, or by hitting the log upon which the bird perched.

The answer? None of the above. Slow-motion movies clearly showed that the wings struck, with each sound-producing beat, only air.

The explosive roar that accompanies the wingbeats of a Ruffed Grouse launching into sudden flight may startle and distract predators. The wings create the sound as they beat below the bird. In the case of the Spruce Grouse and its handsome Asian relative, the Siberian Grouse, the wings clap together above the back. The Rock Dove, or pigeon, familiar in most cities around the world, also claps its wings above its back.

Doves, quail, and other species also distract predators by suddenly erupting into flight with a loud whir of wings. Such species tend to be cryptically colored, blending into the earth, dead leaves, or rocks. A predator may see the movement of one or two of the flock but is startled when all of the birds take to the air at once.

Using their tail feathers, the male Spruce Grouse, native to North America, and males of their close relative, the Siberian Grouse, native to northern Asia, will make swishing sounds during the breeding displays. The pointed tail feathers that give the Sharp-tailed Grouse its name, and one of its most distinctive identifying features, are rattled by the male in breeding displays. The prairie-chickens, with their shorter, broad tail feathers, can quickly snap those feathers open and shut to produce a clicking sound.

Other Grouse Breeding Displays

The Greater Prairie-Chicken's lek display consists of a dance performed with lowered head. During the display, a series of elongated feathers that normally lie compressed and inconspicuous along the sides of the neck are erected over the head, like two stiff horns. Blood flows into the yellow combs above the eyes, causing them to swell. Stiffly held wings are drooped until the primary feathers may brush the ground. The tail is lifted and shaken or abruptly opened and closed. The bird beats out a tattoo on the ground with his feet. The orange or yellowish orange esophageal air

Like their close relative the Sharp-tailed Grouse, the dancing breeding display of the Greater Prairie-Chicken was an inspiration for some of the dances of the Plains Indians of the First Nations.

sacs expand with the compressed air that contributes to the booming sounds that carry out over the prairie in the frosty early-morning air. As if all this were not enough, the male will jump high and frantically flap his wings at the approach of a female, as if in explosive ecstasy. This procedure is called flutter-jumping. Rival males will fight to get above each other in these displays.

Mad-looking flight exhibitions characterize breeding displays of other grouse, including the Spruce Grouse, which may act oblivious to human observers if it is convinced that it is standing near a male rival. Eurasian Black Grouse have similar flight displays.

Pheasants (Family Phasianidae)

The world's best-known Galliforme is a pheasant, although it is seldom recognized as such—the domestic chicken. The various forms of this species of poultry derive from the Red Junglefowl, a boldly patterned and richly colored native of southern Asia. In its natural habitat, the Red Junglefowl is found from northern and northeastern India east through southern China as far as Vietnam, and south to southern Sumatra, Java, and Bali, plus other islands where it may have been introduced by humans in prehistoric times. Some domestic breeds, particularly those unfortunate ones produced to lead pathetic lives of meat or egg production in massive farming operations, are but a faint shadow of these magnificent pheasants in their tropical forest homes. Others are spectacularly ornamental, bred to produce extremes of color, size, and plumage structure.

In rural farming areas around the world, the crowing of the rooster at dawn is a familiar sound. It is fundamentally the same sound heard in the steaming jungles of southeast Asia, where the cock Red Junglefowl crows to challenge other males and attract hens. It is the Red Junglefowl that is the progenitor of all domestic chickens. Children are taught that the rooster sings *cockle-doodle-do* or, to be a little more accurate, *cockle-doodle dooooo*. The wild junglefowl's call is a little higher pitched than that of most domestic roosters, and the final note ends abruptly. It is still clearly identifiable as the call of the rooster. The familiar call, heard at dawn and at other times of the day or night, serves the same purpose as a songbird's song, proclaiming territory and attracting mates.

In keeping with other social members of the family, the Red Junglefowl has an extensive repertoire of calls serving a variety of functions, including keeping contact with the chicks as they accompany the hen through bamboo thickets and jungle clearings. There are three other species of junglefowl, the Gray (India), the Ceylon (Sri Lanka), and the Green (Java).

Argus Pheasants

Less well known than the display of the Indian Peafowl, or peacock, but equally spectacular, are the audio and visual displays of the Great Argus,

In the jungles of southeast Asia, the Red Junglefowl's crowing call is very like the dawn call of the rooster. It's not surprising, as the junglefowl, a species of pheasant, is the progenitor of the domestic chicken.

another large pheasant with very specialized plumage. The inner flight feathers are greatly elongated, as are the central tail plumes. The bird, at the height of the visual display in a forest clearing, can twist its spread wings to form a great fan. The feathers, although lacking the peafowl's dazzling colors, are boldly dotted and barred in intricate patterns throughout their length, and throughout most of the bird's body plumage, as well. It is the loudest pheasant, and its far-carrying wailing cry is one of the most distinctive sounds of the Malaysian and Indonesian rain forests. The sound can be heard up to several kilometers.

Turkeys (Family Meleagrididae)

The white domestic turkey, dragging soil-stained feathers in the barnyard mud as he puffs and struts with spread tail, is engaging in an act designed to display brilliance that has been bred to oblivion. The wild progenitor, slimmer than the domesticated fowl, is famous for the spread tail, swollen body, and the startling *gobble gobble gobble* of his mating display. The Wild Turkey has been found to utter at least twenty-eight different vocalizations. Little attempt has been made to catalogue the corresponding calls of the only other member of the turkey family, the beautiful Ocellated Turkey of the tropical forests of Mexico and Central America.

New World Quails (Family Odontophoridae)

Although the Odontophorids, the New World quails, have a rather simple tracheal syrinx, the calls of some of the species are distinctive and evocative of the regions they inhabit. The *b'-bh, bah-WHITE* of the Common Bobwhite can be heard in suitable open field, hedgerow, and pine barren habitat throughout the southeastern United States. In California, a call the late Roger Tory Peterson described as *qua-QUER-go* or *chi-CA-go* marks the presence of the ubiquitous California Quail in open areas and oak scrublands throughout much of the state. It is quite similar to the call of the very closely related Gambel's Quail of the deserts of the American Southwest and adjoining Mexico.

Chachalacas, Curassows, and Guans (Family Cracidae)

Like the turkeys and the New World quails, a family of large birds, the Cracids, is confined to the Western Hemisphere, mostly the tropics and

The Wild Turkey has been recorded producing at least 28 distinct vocalizations.

subtropics, although a few species are found in higher latitudes in both the Northern and Southern Hemispheres. The Plain Chachalaca is found mostly in Mexico, although there is a small, isolated population as far south as Costa Rica, and the northern edge of the range reaches the southern tip of Texas. When a flock starts vocalizing, it is the noisiest fauna of the acacia thickets along the edges of the lower Rio Grande. The *cha-cha-ca* that gives the bird its name is often hard to discern among a chorus of grunts, squeals, squawks, and other raucous noises.

Related to the various species of chachalacas, but more similar to them than to the curassows, are sleek, long-necked, long-tailed birds called guans. Found in tropical South America, the most singular of the guans, both in appearance and in vocalization, is the Horned Guan. Its voice has been called noticeably ventriloquial. The mooing three or four soft, low notes give no accurate clue as to the bird's location. More typical is the Spix's Guan, also native to tropical South America, which utters loud, discordant, and far-carrying hoarse notes. Members of the genus *Pipile,* called piping-guans, characteristically utter a series of thin, high-pitched calls.

For all the interesting aspects of their varied vocalizations, among Cracids the guans are particularly known for their mechanical sounds. Again, the aberrant Horned Guan is an exception, so far as we know, but the other guans perform unusual wing drumming or wing-whirring flights. These are performed very early in the morning. Although some guans may make wing-whirring flights at various times of the year, they are clearly associated with breeding.

The performance usually begins when the guan launches himself from a perch above the forest canopy or overlooking a clearing. The bird briefly glides on outstretched wings, then suddenly, for about three seconds, furiously beats the wings at far faster than the normal rate of speed, then continues with the glide, to another exposed perch.

The actual brief period of whirring consists of two segments, separated by a fraction of a second. In the first part, the wingbeats accelerate, then there is an abrupt stop and very brief pause. The wings instantly start again at about the rate of acceleration where they left off, but they slow down. The bird may repeat this display several times in one session, always flying to and from different perches.

The first time I heard the sound of the Yellow-knobbed Curassow, I was a little nonplussed. It seemed somehow the wrong kind of song to come from such a large bird. The call I heard was a long, thin whistle with a slight lowering of tone near the end. It has been likened to the sound of a bomb falling, just prior to detonation.

The very closely related Wattled Curassow has a similar song. Other related curassows, all members of the genus *Crax*, can use whistled notes for other reasons, such as alarm, but employ deep, closed-mouthed, booming sounds as their territorial songs.

THIRTEEN

Woodpeckers

It is early March in a deciduous woodlot in Vermont. The air is cold, but there is a welcome spring warmth to the sun as it filters through bare branches of oaks, beech trees, black cherries, and maples. Bloodroot blooms amid dirty patches of snow. In the distance is the cawing of crows. Suddenly there is a rapid-fire staccato burst of drumming at the rate of nine to sixteen times per second. Such staccato drum rolls can be heard from other parts of the woods, near and far. Each is an affirmation of territorial claim made by a small black and white bird called the Downy Woodpecker. Both sexes engage in drumming. Possibly North America's most common and widely distributed woodpecker, the Downy's drumming can be as much a harbinger of spring as the boisterous singing of a Song Sparrow or an American Robin's caroling. From the birds' standpoint, it serves much the same purposes of establishing territory and attracting mates.

The very similar, but slightly larger, Hairy Woodpecker is found in many of the same forests and woods as the Downy. The Hairy has a drum roll of similar duration, but it is faster and often tends to slow down at the end. The Black-backed Woodpecker shares some of the same range and habitat as the Downy and Hairy Woodpeckers, in northern North America. Its drum rolls are slower than those of the Hairy Woodpecker and tend to accelerate at the end. The Three-toed Woodpecker is closely related to the Black-backed but is only about half as long. It shares much of its habitat but is also found throughout much of northern and central Eurasia. Its drum roll, performed by either sex, is slower and shorter than the corresponding sound made by the Black-backed Woodpecker. The drum roll of the Three-toed resembles that of the much larger Black Woodpecker, with which it shares woodland habitat in parts of Eurasia. Such differences are

parts of a suite of characteristics, including vocalizations, appearance, and habitat, that serve as isolating mechanisms among the woodpeckers.

Woodpeckers not only gather food with their beaks, but they use the beaks to communicate. Instead of singing, they hammer or drum, often picking a specially resonating surface to do so. The tin roof of a shed may have acoustical characteristics that work quite well for some species, such as the Acorn Woodpecker of western North America and Central America. A log or tree trunk or the siding of a house may be chosen specifically because it produces a loud sound. These special drumming surfaces come to serve as song perches do for oscines.

A Pileated Woodpecker, hammering on a tree trunk, strikes the trunk thirty-two times every one and a half seconds. The larger Ivory-billed Woodpecker, native to the southeastern United Sates and Cuba, gives a highly distinctive double tap—or did; the species is almost certainly now extinct, although rumors of its survival occasionally persist.

In hammering, the woodpecker's beak strikes with great speed, around 6 or 7 meters per second. The beak impacts directly at right angles, the eyes closing a fraction of a second before contact. Stiff bristles, which are specially modified feathers, cover the nostrils to protect the bird from inhaling wood chips and dust. The energy generated by the impact of beak against the surface is more widely distributed through the bony structures and soft anatomy of the head, relative to the amount of the head taken up by the brain, than is true of humans. Indeed, it's been estimated that the woodpecker's brain is fifty to one hundred times less vulnerable to damage from the forces generated by hammering than would be a human brain subjected to similar forces. Much of the shock is directed away from the woodpecker's brain.

Woodpecker Vocalizations

Scientists have taken one group of woodpeckers, members of the genus *Picoides,* and examined their calls with a view of categorizing them. This genus is found in many parts of the world and includes the Downy, Hairy, Three-toed, and Black-backed Woodpeckers, plus numerous other species. The categories of sounds identified among the *Picoides* woodpeckers may be more or less applicable to all woodpeckers. Loud, conspicuous calls

Characteristics of its drum roll help identify the Black Woodpecker, native to Eurasia.

help maintain contact between individuals, as do the long-distance calls, which are usually loud, rattling noises. In lacking the sophisticated and complex anatomical control over vocalization found in the songbirds, such calls usually consist of a rapidly uttered series of more or less similar notes, with variation between the species provided by loudness, frequency, and duration of the overall call. Some calls are related to breeding and may be associated with aerial displays with fluttering wings, not unlike those of a lark, but far less likely to evoke poetic musings. Nestlings also give a variety of calls, some rudimentary forms of the calls they will give as adults.

When woodpeckers challenge each other, many species use the familiar *wika* or *weka* calls, often heard from the Northern Flicker, a colorful woodpecker regularly encountered in parks and gardens in North America. Such calls customarily accompany ritualistic displays of bowing and swaying, skyward beak-pointing, and perhaps partial wing and tail openings that reveal underwing patterns—bright yellow in eastern birds, salmon red in the west.

There are also intimate calls between individuals and typically associated with precopulation or nesting duties. A woodpecker's vocal repertoire includes the raucous distress calls familiar to anyone who has taken a woodpecker in hand. Boldness and noisy conflicts between species sometimes occur. Indeed, one of the most colorful, noisy avian spats I ever saw involved a member of the western race of the Northern Flicker arguing with both a Pileated Woodpecker and a Lewis's Woodpecker, in southern British Columbia. All three flew about, yelled noisily, seemed to be absolutely annoyed, and did no harm whatsoever.

Nuthatches

The nuthatch family, Sittidae, is a remarkably homogeneous assembly of small songbirds with strong feet, short and softly feathered tails, straight beaks, and a habit of crawling about on trees and branches or even rocks. Often they are seen climbing downward, headfirst, probing for insects and performing acrobatic maneuvers that include hanging upside down from the undersides of branches.

Nuthatches are named for their ability to place a nut or seed into a crevice and then pound it open. An aberrant member of the family is the colorful Wallcreeper, an Old World species that crawls about on rocks and cliffs, probing for food with a long, slender, straight beak. The Wallcreeper's thin calls and not unmusical whistles are as atypical of other nuthatches as is the bird's overall appearance. Its full song is quite spectacular, and has been described as ". . . an ascending series of 4–5 clear, piping whistled units in a gradually slowing sequence, the individual notes sometimes slightly rising in pitch, *zee-zee-zee-zee-swee,* followed by a prolonged (c. 1 second), lower pitched and very quiet note, given only in full song." There are often incomplete versions of the song, and ". . . the mountain acoustics help the song to sound loud and powerful . . ." if it is not drowned out by the sound of wind or rushing water.

Other nuthatches generally have some variant of the short, nasal calls of such familiar species as the Eurasian Nuthatch in the Old World and the White-breasted Nuthatch of temperate North America.

However, nuthatches also have quite musical, if understated, abilities to sing in a series of chortling whistles and warbles that are unlike their more familiar call notes. And although they do not drum as do woodpeckers, the sound of them hammering open a hard-shelled delicacy, such as a sunflower seed, is certainly audible.

Treecreepers

The treeceepers are members of the songbird family Certhiidae. The two best-known members of the family, the Brown Creeper of North and Central America and the widely distributed Eurasian Treecreeper, are so very similar to each other that they were once considered the same species. They are two of a small assembly of members of the genus *Certhia.* These are tiny birds, generally light-colored below, streaked in brown and white above, with intricately patterned wings colored in shades of blackish-brown, tan, and white.

The songs of the treecreepers tend to be thin, perhaps a little buzzy, and high-pitched. To varying degrees, where ranges overlap they show an ability to learn the songs of other species of treecreepers, sometimes perfectly! As some species have wide ranges and much geographic variation, not surprisingly, the songs and calls within a species may vary somewhat geographically, in the form of regional accents. These tiny birds cannot make pounding noises with their delicate beaks. Their songs, and the birds themselves, are often overlooked in the woods and forests the birds inhabit.

FOURTEEN

Cranes

This family of long-legged, long-necked birds, family Gruidae, order Gruiiformes, consists of fifteen species widely distributed in North America, Eurasia, Africa, and Australia.

Whatever the species, a crane's vocabulary begins with an entirely instinctive and highly functional peeping, heard from hatchlings and continuing through the first year. Within a day of hatching, the baby birds instinctively utter a purring contact call, which, in its more intense forms, indicates a need for parental attention. Also within a day or so of hatching, the birds start low-pitched food begging calls. As they mature, the young birds add still more calls, signaling intention to fly, or alarm.

These calls of the young birds vary little among the various species. Indeed, one conservation strategy that has been attempted on behalf of enhancing numbers of wild Whooping Cranes has been cross-fostering— the placement of Whooping Crane eggs into nests of the relatively common Sandhill Crane. At least in the early stages of crane development, visual and audio signals are so similar that the ruse works.

New calls begin to develop as young cranes mature and start to diverge from calls relatively common to all crane hatchlings. These various calls signal or reinforce diverse intentions or initiatives.

Breeding displays of some species, such as the Whooping Crane or the gray-colored Sandhill Crane, are accompanied by a dancing display that sees the birds leaping about, wings spread or flopping, legs gangling, as the birds jump high into the air. Visitors driving through the Central Valley of California, in the fields near the Sacramento Delta region, can easily view the Sandhills' high-spirited dance from the edge of farm roads. It's a display that is highly ritualistic and of ancient lineage.

Some other, smaller crane species have somewhat less spectacular calls and cries, including the booming noises of the Gray and the Black Crowned Cranes of Africa, and the raspier, unmusical calls of the smaller and quite elegant Blue Crane, also native to Africa.

Whooping Cranes and the Quality of Wildness

One of my more thrilling moments in the close company of birds came through the gracious courtesy of the International Crane Foundation, in Baraboo, Wisconsin. The foundation is admirably involved in many aspects of crane conservation worldwide, often assisting various countries to develop educational programs on crane conservation and protection, but it is perhaps best known for its successful captive crane breeding and release program.

I visited the foundation in the late winter and was taken behind the scenes, to spacious pens that held many family groups and breeding pairs of cranes. I was invited into enclosures holding breeding pairs of Whooping Cranes. No other species better epitomizes endangerment and the human struggle against all odds to fight to protect such critically endangered species.

In 1941, only fifteen Whooping Cranes were counted on their wintering grounds in Texas. That appeared to be the world's entire population. Now there are at least ten times that number, thanks to a massive binational, long-term, costly, high-profile conservation effort by the private and public sectors. The species is still endangered, but it looks like it just might be saved.

One of my hosts at the International Crane Foundation, Scott Swengel, asked if I'd like to hear the Whooping Cranes whoop up close. The birds were not used to me, and it is impossible to imagine quite what they made either of me or of other humans. To entice the pair in the first enclosure we entered to whoop, Scott did a superb Whooping Crane imitation. The male responded, going into a dramatic display, wings drooping, head up, mouth open, and uttering his loud, discordant, wonderfully wild whooping call. The female then responded to the male with her own version of the same call, uttered several times to each call of her mate, her calls

The male begins the wonderfully wild whooping call of the Whooping Crane, but before he completes the call the slightly smaller female has joined in. Few sounds better evoke the wildness still to be found in North America.

shorter in length and starting before the male's initial *whooooop* was complete. Scott had started something.

What was happening was a primal form of duet calling, known as unison calling. It is considered to be primal because essentially the notes are similar, the whole of it consisting of first Scott, then the male, then the female calling, in distinction from duets, where one part of a complex vocalization is uttered by one bird, to be completed by the other, to form a seamless whole. The unison calling of cranes probably serves several purposes, functioning to help reinforce pair bonding while establishing breeding territory and challenging other males. The female's call is slightly more highly pitched than that of the males.

FIFTEEN

The Ubiquitous Presence of Sound

Once I discovered absolute soundlessness while I stood on a sun-baked pan in the Kalahari Desert, in midday. A bush-robin occasionally sang a partial song in the distance, but when that bird was silent, I heard utterly nothing.

Then I began to hear a squeaking. I couldn't tell where the noise, which seemed to surround me, was coming from. A mouse? A small bird? Some odd insect? It was none of those things; it was the strap of my binoculars, a sound so quiet that in all the thousands of hours I had worn them, it had never before been so silent that I could hear that sound. The absence of all other sound compelled awareness of the one faint sound that remained, my binocular strap. A Batleur Eagle sailed by overhead, and as I watched it, I had a strange sensation that I was both standing in and viewing a full-color, three-dimensional movie with the sound turned off. It occurred to me that as the eagle soared, it must hear the passage of air through the great feathers of its wings.

I recall a summer evening beside a rural road with two friends who were going to introduce me to a bird usually found by its song, if you know what to listen for. The species, the Henslow's Sparrow, was rare then and has since become so much rarer that it has been placed on the endangered species list for my region. It is an unobtrusive little bird that is normally found in long grass and weedy tangles. Ah, but the song, rendered just at twilight, gives it away.

No Nightingale this, the Henslow's Sparrow has one of the most abrupt songs of any songbird in the world. Its call is an unobtrusive, somewhat insectlike, double-noted *tse-slick,* also rendered *tsi-lick* or *flee-sic.*

Few birdsongs are more easily overlooked, and those who have heard—and known that they have heard—the call of the Henslow's Sparrow are few indeed.

There is a little more to this modest bird, however. I referred to the sound I heard as a call, because that is the impression it gives, but the brief vocalization is actually the song, packing into its relatively few utterances and short length all that a songbird's song is supposed to convey by means of establishing and maintaining territory and attracting a mate. The Henslow's Sparrow actually does have a flight song, a modest effort, rarely heard, and consisting of a series of short, quickly uttered notes. It will never be the stuff of poetry, but it does help define this entity we have named the Henslow's Sparrow, native to the fields of eastern North America—a few of them, at any rate, where it goes about its business mostly unseen and unheard. Henslow's Sparrows sing for Henslow's Sparrows, not for humans. We listen in.

Each species has its own degree of reliance on any of the senses. There is not just one world as perceived by us, but multiple, overlapping worlds, each varying to some degree. A banana slug on the floor of a California redwood forest is part of that forest and experiences things about that forest that you and I can never detect, and yet the invertebrate does not even know there is a forest, as we define "knowing." We may know there is a forest but can easily be oblivious to the banana slug. We may hear the sighing of wind in the tops of the redwoods and recognize what it is, while the jumbling, tinkling notes of a Winter Wren's song remain nothing more than a background sound, appropriate, but not appreciated as to purpose or origin or complexity.

But such indifference is not in our own best interest if that interest is to include a fuller appreciation of all that is worthy of appreciating. We are part of the whole that includes the redwoods, the slug, and the wren. And unlike the slug, we and the wren can think. And far more than the wren, we can understand, analyze, and appreciate. Most of all, perhaps, we can simply enjoy, with all our senses, a richly complex and infinitely intricate book of mysteries.

SUGGESTED READINGS

Written material used in writing this book included scientific papers published in peer-review journals, a wide variety of technical and non-technical books, and a few newspaper articles. Among books referred to were some generalized books about either certain taxa (groups of related birds) or birds of certain regions, including field guides and regional handbooks. Older books, now out of print and difficult to find in libraries, were also sometimes used as a source of information.

There are numerous CD ROMs, CDs, and audio tapes featuring bird-songs of various regions, with new titles continually added. Additionally, the Internet has a wide (and growing) variety of sites dealing with various aspects of ornithology. In addition to printed information, there are numerous bird images and sounds available to anyone who takes the time to surf the net. Perhaps the best starting point to begin such surfing is Denis LePage's comprehensive Bird Links to the World page at www.ntic.qc.ca/~nellus/links.html.

The following is a brief list of books that are either broadly generalist in covering the field of ornithology, or specific to bird sound, and should be in print or available through the library. They are only the tip of the iceberg in terms of the printed information available about birds, but they're a good start to further reading about birds and bird sounds.

Catchpole, C. K., and P. J. B. Slater. *Bird Song: Biological Themes and Variations*. New York: Press Syndicate of the University of Cambridge, 1985. (Although rather technical, this is an easily understood overview of research into birdsong and, like Jellis [below], an excellent in-depth continuation into areas more briefly explored in the current volume.)

Ford, Barbara. *How Birds Learn to Sing*. New York: Julian Messner, 1975. (A charming non-technical exploration of many of the most important researches into birdsong production.)

Gill, Frank B. *Ornithology,* 2nd Edition. New York: W. H. Freeman and Company, 1994. (An excellent non-technical and very comprehensive review of ornithology.)

Jardine, Ernie. *Bird Song Identification Made Easy*. Toronto: Natural Heritage/Natural History, Inc., 1996. (Virtually all bird guides provide descriptions of birdsongs, but for birders in temperate eastern North America, this is an excellent book to actually teach the identification, by sound alone, of 125 species quite likely to be encountered in the region.)

Jellis, Rosemary. *Bird Sounds and Their Meanings*. Ithaca: Cornell University Press, 1997. (Somewhat technical, but easily understood by the adult reader, this book emerged from a series of lectures presented on radio by the British Broadcasting Corporation, and explores in depth many aspects of bird sound production in general, and songbird vocalization in particular. Like Catchpole and Slater [above], this book is an excellent continuation from the current volume.)

Kroodsma, Donald E., and Edward H. Miller, Eds. *Ecology and Evolution of Acoustic Communication in Birds*. Ithaca: Cornell University Press, 1996. (An extensive assembly of often highly technical papers by numerous scientists dealing with various aspects of avian vocalizations; not suitable for the lay reader but an essential reference for anyone with advanced interest in the subject.)

Ornestein, Ronald. *Songbirds of the World, Celebrating Nature's Voices*. Toronto: Key Porter Books Limited, 1997. (An excellent non-technical examination of world songbird biology.)

Rising, Trudy and Jim. *Canadian Songbirds and Their Ways*. Montreal: Tundra Books, 1982.

Terres, John K. *The Audubon Society Encyclopedia of North American Birds*. New York: Alfred A. Knopf, Inc., 1980. (A non-technical reference with interesting and well-presented material relating to many aspects of bird study, including bird sound.)

Currently being published and of particular value and inspiration in better understanding birds, their diversity, and their biology—including excellent discussions of vocalizations at the family level—is the multi-volume series *Handbook of Birds of the World*, edited by Joseph del Hoyo, Andrew Elliott, and Jordi Sargatal, and published by Lynx Ediciones, Barcelona, for Birdlife International, starting with Volume 1, published in 1992. Volume 5 was published in 1999, with more volumes to be produced in the future until all bird species have been covered.

Additionally, what is popularly known as the "Helm Series" of books describing families of birds, variously published by Pica Press, Princeton University Press, and Houghton Mifflin, is a valuable reference and provides the non-technical reader with color illustrations and comprehensive life histories of the world's birds, including extensive description of vocalizations and mechanical sound production. Sample titles include *Nightjars: A Guide to Nightjars and Related Nightbirds*, by Nigel Cleere and Dave Nurney, published by Pica Press, The Banks, Mountfield, Nr. Robertsbridge, East Sussex, U.K. (1998); *Finches & Sparrows: An Identification Guide*, by Peter Clement, Alan Harris, and John Davis, published by Princeton University Press, Princeton, N.J. (1993); and *Shorebirds: An Identification Guide*, by Peter Hayman, John Marchant, and Tony Prater, published by Houghton Mifflin Company, Boston (1986).

INDEX

Page numbers in italics indicate illustrations or sidebars.